Research Series on Responsible Enterprise Ecosystems

Series Editors

Samuel O. Idowu, London Metropolitan University, London, UK

Nadia E. Nedzel, Southern University Law Center, Baton Rouge, USA

Mara Del Baldo, Dept of Economics, Society and Politics, University of Urbino, Urbino, Italy

Adriana Burlea Schiopoiu, Economics and Business Administration, University of Craiova, Dolj, Romania

This book series focuses on sustainability, governance, and diversity in SMEs, small businesses, and startups. The series aims to unlock the potential of sustainability, governance, and diversity within SMEs, fostering a new era of responsible and inclusive entrepreneurship.

Delving into the challenges and opportunities of sustainable practices and governance in these organizations, it provides a platform for scholars, researchers, and practitioners to share their valuable insights and experiences. The series encourages and features innovative approaches, best practices, and real-life case studies, showcasing successful integration of sustainability, governance, and diversity principles. This diverse collection of knowledge will resonate with readers from various backgrounds, including law, management, accounting, CSR practices, and more, encouraging a cross-disciplinary dialogue. From circular economy models to gender diversity initiatives, the books offer pragmatic solutions for sustainable corporate governance. As the world navigates socio-economic and environmental crises, the series also emphasizes the resilience of SMEs in regenerating societies. By championing ethical conduct and inclusiveness, the series envisions SMEs as powerful drivers of positive change.

With each volume maintaining a coherent pedagogy and content style, the series is a must-have resource for educators, managers, entrepreneurs, and scholars alike.

Antonio Baraybar-Fernández
Sandro Arrufat-Martín • Belén Díaz Díaz
Editors

The AI Revolution

How Technological Developments Affect the Audiovisual Sector

Springer

Editors
Antonio Baraybar-Fernández
King Juan Carlos University
Fuenlabrada, Spain

Belén Díaz Díaz
Universidad de Cantabria
Santander, Spain

Sandro Arrufat-Martín
King Juan Carlos University
Fuenlabrada, Spain

International University of La Rioja (UNIR)
La Rioja, Spain

ISSN 3004-8834 ISSN 3004-8842 (electronic)
Research Series on Responsible Enterprise Ecosystems
ISBN 978-3-031-80413-7 ISBN 978-3-031-80411-3 (eBook)
https://doi.org/10.1007/978-3-031-80411-3

This Springer imprint is published by the registered company Springer Nature Switzerland AG
The registered company address is: Gewerbestrasse 11, 6330 Cham, Switzerland

Preface

In a world of constant evolution, few phenomena have captivated the public imagination and debate as intensely as artificial intelligence (AI). The impact of AI extends to all corners of society, but one sector where its influence is particularly dramatic is the audiovisual industry. From film production to digital content creation, AI is transforming not only how audiovisual products are created but also how they are distributed, consumed, and understood.

This book, The AI Revolution: How Can This Revolution Affect the Audiovisual Sector?, seeks to explore these transformations in depth and provide a critical view of the changes that AI is bringing to the audiovisual field. Through a series of chapters written by recognized experts in their respective fields, this volume offers a comprehensive overview of the challenges, opportunities, and ethical dilemmas arising from the integration of AI into this dynamic sector.

Chapter 1: Artificial Intelligence in Audiovisuals: Revolution or Bubble?

Authors Antonio Baraybar-Fernández and Sandro Arrufat-Martín explore whether AI's impact on the communication sector is a true revolution or simply an evolution of existing practices. The chapter analyzes investment needs, potential risks like economic bubbles, and AI's influence on journalism, marketing, and advertising. It emphasizes the importance of research to understand AI's real opportunities and limits while highlighting that technology will enhance, not replace, human decision-making in the sector.

Chapter 2: OpenAI and Bain & Company: A Strategic Alliance to Optimize Technology and Its Applicability

Marina Rodríguez Hernández, Paloma Fernández Fernández, and Miguel Baños González explore the strategic collaboration between OpenAI and Bain & Company. This chapter analyzes how these alliances are optimizing AI technology and its applicability in the audiovisual sector, and how these partnerships may influence the future of the industry.

Chapter 3: Ethical Considerations in the Use of Artificial Intelligence in the Audiovisual Industry

Rebeca-Illiana Arévalo-Martínez, Rogelio Del Prado Flores, and Ricardo Ignacio Prado Hurtado offer a critical reflection on the ethical implications of using AI in the audiovisual industry. The chapter addresses issues such as responsibility, transparency, and the social impact of emerging technologies.

Chapter 4: Implication of Artificial Intelligence in the Study Area of Neurocommunication and Media Literacy

In this chapter, Almudena Barrientos-Báez, David Caldevilla-Domínguez, and Felipe Chibás Ortiz explore how AI is influencing neurocommunication and media literacy. This analysis examines how new technologies affect the way we process and understand audiovisual information.

Chapter 5: Creativity in the AI Revolution

Jesús Plaza investigates how AI is redefining creativity in the audiovisual sector. This chapter examines the role of AI in generating innovative content and how creatives are adapting their workflows in response to these new tools.

Chapter 6: Ethical and Legal Challenges of Artificial Intelligence with Respect to Fundamental Rights: The Protection of Privacy and Intellectual Property

Patricia Lalanda and Neus Alcolea address the ethical and legal challenges posed by AI concerning fundamental rights, including privacy protection and intellectual property. This chapter provides a detailed view of the legal issues arising from AI integration in audiovisual production.

Chapter 7: Artificial Intelligence and Communication: The Threat of Deepfakes

Lucas Morales Domínguez, José Luis Zurita Andión, and Malgorzata Kolankowska explore the impact of deepfakes on communication. This chapter analyzes how AI technologies are used to create false content and the associated risks for credibility and information security.

Chapter 8: Generative Artificial Intelligence Applied to Audiovisual Production: Emerging Languages and Techniques

Mario Rajas and Manuel Gértrudix examine how generative AI is being applied to audiovisual production. This chapter analyzes the new languages and emerging techniques that are redefining the creative and production processes in the industry.

Through this collection of studies and analyses, we hope to provide a comprehensive understanding of how AI is influencing the audiovisual sector. This book not only offers an evaluation of current trends but also raises critical questions about the industry's future and the role AI will play in its evolution. As we enter this transformative era, it is essential to reflect on the implications of these technologies and prepare for the changes that lie ahead.

Fuenlabrada, Spain Antonio Baraybar-Fernández
Fuenlabrada, Spain Sandro Arrufat-Martín
La Rioja, Spain
Santander, Spain Belén Díaz Díaz
September 2024

Contents

About the Editors

Antonio Baraybar-Fernández Full Professor of Audiovisual Communication and Advertising at the Rey Juan Carlos University. Ph.D. in Information Sciences from the Complutense University of Madrid. Member of the high-performance research group at URJC: INFOCENT. His research interests are related to Communication Economics, Communication Management in Organizations, and Neuroscience applied to Communication. He has published his studies and research in prestigious international and Spanish publishing houses, as well as in academic journals indexed in the world's leading databases. He has served as the Vice-Dean of Technology and Resources for the Faculty of Communication Sciences and as the head of the Department of Communication and Sociology Sciences at URJC. He has also been the director of the Francisco Villamartín chair (CESEDEN-URJC).

Sandro Arrufat-Martín, Cum Laude Doctor in Communication Sciences from the Rey Juan Carlos University (2021). Master in Protocol, Communication and Comprehensive Organization of Events from the URJC (2018) and Master in Corporate Communication Management from EAE Business School (2017). Bachelor's Degree in Journalism from UDIMA (2016). Currently, associate professor at the Rey Juan Carlos University, having won a competitive contest in the Department of Audiovisual Communication and Advertising. He teaches at both undergraduate and master's levels at the International University of La Rioja (UNIR), EAE Business School and the Madrid Chamber of Commerce. In addition, he is the author of journals indexed in the Arts & Humanities Citation Index (A&HCI) of Web of Science, Scopus, Emerging Sources Citation Index (ESCI), Latindex, among others. He has also published book chapters included in Scholarly Publishers Indicators (SPI). In addition, he has been involved in various research projects related to digital communication management and strategies, social networks and corporate reputation. Likewise, his research areas include public relations, branding and corporate communication.

Belén Díaz Díaz is Ph.D. in Finance. She is Associate Professor of Finance at the University of Cantabria (Spain) and Academic Director at Santander Financial Institute (SANFI). Previously, she has been Vice-Dean of the Faculty of Economics and Business Administration and Director of Campus and Social Development at the University of Cantabria. She has been visiting researcher at the University of California in Berkeley, the London School of Economics, the University of Technology in Sydney, and at different universities in Mexico, Chile, Brazil, Argentina and Morocco. Professor Díaz is author of several papers about CSR, Corporate Governance, banking and corporate finance in academic journals and books. The quality of her research was recognized with the "Sanchis Alcover Award", awarded by the Scientific Association of Economy and Management in 2006. Since 1996, she has written several reports and developed more than 50 R&D projects about different financial and economic issues commissioned by different public and private entities.

Chapter 1
OpenAI Artificial Intelligence: Revolution or Bubble?

Antonio Baraybar-Fernández and Sandro Arrufat-Martín

1.1 Introduction

“Mirror, mirror on my wall! Who is the fairest of them all?” This popular phrase from the Evil Queen in the tale of Snow White appears in the Brothers Grimm version from the eighteenth century. In this second decade of the twenty-first century, in an updated version aligned with our social practices, it wouldn’t be far-fetched to imagine that this magical mirror could be replaced by a query to ChatGPT. However, the response from its free version at the time of writing this chapter might leave us somewhat unsatisfied by breaking the narrative conflict—that is, the story’s tension between good and evil, embodied in a beautiful, yet proud and arrogant woman: “Everyone has their own unique beauty. True beauty is within.”

Referring to this tale in the introductory paragraph aims to highlight the fundamental idea of this chapter: to view Generative Artificial Intelligence (Gen AI) as a resource rather than an oracle, even though it is becoming increasingly sophisticated and its results can evoke a certain fascination. It is a tool for accessing information and establishing a dialogue that accompanies and assists in the search for creative solutions, generating novel ideas, or automating processes that reduce costs and increase competitiveness. For AI to succeed, it must avoid representations inspired by the world of science fiction created around computers. Its goal should not be for users to obtain a correct answer as quickly and easily as possible, but

A. Baraybar-Fernández (✉)
Department of Communication and Sociology, King Juan Carlos University, Móstoles, Spain
e-mail: antonio.baraybar@urjc.es

S. Arrufat-Martín
Department of Communication and Sociology, King Juan Carlos University, Móstoles, Spain

International University of La Rioja (UNIR), Logroño, Spain
e-mail: sandro.arrufat@urjc.es; sandro.arrufat@unir.net

A. Baraybar-Fernández et al. (eds.), *The AI Revolution*, Research Series on Responsible Enterprise Ecosystems, https://doi.org/10.1007/978-3-031-80411-3_1

rather to support their capabilities and enhance their understanding of the challenges they face in the real world (Shah & Bender, 2024: 19).

Historians like André Jolles and Georges Dumézil place storytelling at the origin of culture (Piglia, 2011, p. 15). Philosopher Karl Popper proposed that the most characteristic feature of human language is the ability to tell stories, suggesting that the moment language became human is closely related to the moment when man invented a tale (Popper, 1974). Today, storytellers can rely on new technology, not be replaced by it. If a screenwriter accustomed to regularly using ChatGPT had asked the Evil Queen's question from Snow White, the response would have been different, and through dialogue with the tool—already trained according to their interests—it would have opened up new possibilities in constructing the narrative conflict essential to any story.

The countless possibilities opened up by large language models (LLMs), with their numerous ramifications, promise a paradigmatic cultural shift. Amid the shifting sands caused by an incessant flow of information in the media and on social networks, divergent opinions and reflections on Artificial Intelligence (AI) are emerging in academia in an embryonic form, focusing on the opportunities and threats posed by this new technology.

There is a socially influential discourse predicting a revolution similar to those triggered by other scientific advancements like the steam engine, electricity, computing, or the internet, driven by AI (Sheikh et al., 2023). For now, AI has moved beyond the realm of fantasy, and its application impacts various productive sectors, including those related to information and communication (López-García, 2024). In an interview published in MIT Technology Review in May 2023, Geoffrey Hinton, one of the pioneers of deep learning, expressed his concern about the potential misuse of the tools he helped create. Among other issues, he highlighted their ability to manipulate citizens in elections and wars or reinforce social inequality. In contrast, Yann LeCun, who shared the Turing Award with Hinton in 2018, predicts "a new renaissance of humanity." It is likely that generative AI may undergo a process similar to what happened with the internet, from which it has inherited unresolved issues and problems like biases in data interpretation or manipulation through bots. Once the foundational generative models from OpenAI, Google, Meta, and possibly others establish an effective infrastructure (enablers), its full potential may not be realized until thousands of users experiment with it.

1.2 Is There a Risk of an Economic Bubble in the Field of AI?

Money is not synonymous with innovation, but it is essential for ensuring that an innovation has widespread social use. The more players that invest in AI and its potential, the greater the chances for prosperous development. It is not advisable to view AI simply as a value chain encompassing everything from microchip industries (e.g., Nvidia) to data platforms or cloud services (e.g., Microsoft, Amazon, Google …). Many other companies across different sectors will seek to leverage the opportunities provided by this technology. For instance, companies like Meta or Instagram, which have demonstrated adeptness at engaging with Generation Z, aim to generate user-specific advertising. Beyond the companies creating the platforms, other sectors or sub-sectors are involved in this apparent revolution. For AI expansion to become a reality, significant investments, including public sector funding, are necessary to build large data processing centers, which require substantial electrical resources for operation and water resources for cooling.

In their first-quarter 2024 earnings reports, many tech companies, such as Microsoft, Amazon, and Alphabet, have placed AI at the core of their growth strategy. Recently, there has been a significant increase in the demand for data centers, with no signs of stabilization in the short term. For illustration, OpenAI's GPT-2 model had about two million parameters, while OpenAI's GPT-4 operates with approximately 1.7 trillion parameters, although OpenAI has not officially confirmed these figures.

The need to train and develop more complex generative models requires robust infrastructures to build powerful models and extensive low-latency inference capabilities to effectively deploy applications in the real world. In this context, digital sovereignty is starting to play a significant role. It is no longer just about the location of data storage and processing but also about the type of data used to train models. Governments and companies are aware of the importance of training these models according to their own regulations and cultural norms, rather than relying on a globally generalized model based solely on cost efficiency or location.

It is prudent to be cautious about a discourse with high expectations driven by the major companies leading this technology. Some research suggests that AI systems may pursue strategic interests, such as pleasing users, rather than strictly focusing on accuracy (Park et al., 2024). The regular behavior patterns they use can lead to the creation of false beliefs. Therefore, there is a need to disclose when interacting with an AI chatbot or to identify images and videos with watermarks, although, as has been shown, these can currently be easily removed or falsified (Li et al., 2024).

The value of developing this technology will be quantified when its acceptance in professional and public spheres begins to yield returns on the significant investments made, which will need to be sustained in the short term. In other words, when it demonstrates its ability to meet users' needs. Many professionals recognize AI's potential to increase efficiency, and 40% expecting it to significantly transform their professions within the next 5 years; new skills will be required, necessitating training in a new culture of learning (PwC, 2024). In the current development phase, as with other technologies, early adopters and enthusiasts are the most proactive in seeking their own training, often using less regulated and verified sources. However, if its application indeed translates into improved business competitiveness, companies will need to promote training, which could also become a crucial factor in attracting and retaining talent.

The term "economic or financial bubble" lacks a universally agreed-upon definition (Siegel, 2003); however, it is associated with the unsustainable rise in the price of an asset due to excessive speculation. In other words, the increase in the asset's value is not based on classical economic arguments, such as strong guarantees of benefits, future income, intrinsic value, or need (Quinn & Turner, 2020). A bubble forms around a triple axis: a rapid and continuous increase in prices driven by high expectations of future profits, high investor participation, and an asset price linked to expectations or promises not supported by verifiable economic data, thus carrying evident risk. If this situation cannot be maintained indefinitely and the expected results are not met, a sharp price drop or crash often occurs, frequently leading to a financial crisis (Kindleberger, 2016).

Following the dot-com bubble (1997–2001), it seems timely to consider whether these key elements are being replicated today and assess the risks of a new bubble forming. AI has undoubtedly been one of the major trends gaining prominence in 2024. Since OpenAI introduced ChatGPT on November 30, 2022, interest in AI has surged dramatically among specialized audiences and the general public. Nine years after OpenAI was founded in San Francisco, it has become the leading company in this technology, with The New York Times reporting a valuation of $80 billion (Metz et al., 2023).

This chatbot, capable of providing answers to a wide range of questions from text prompts, surpassed 100 million active monthly users in just 2 months. This achievement made it the fastest platform to reach this milestone, although Meta's Threads app improved upon these results in July. According to specialized press data, investment could approach $125 billion, with estimates predicting a 50% increase by the end of 2024, reaching $184 billion.

The business results of related products also raise expectations; for example, microchips, essential for equipping modern data processing centers where new AI algorithms are trained. Nvidia's growth exemplifies this trend, influencing a very positive valuation of major AI-related stocks. Nvidia chip prices have risen alongside their processing capacity, with new models speculated to be priced between $30,000 and $40,000, and a waiting list in place. Meanwhile, the company's stock price has tripled over the past year, disconnected from classical economic fundamentals. Given the many investments being made in startups by venture capital, the previously mentioned points about a potential financial bubble appear to be manifesting.

Comparing the current situation to the dot-com crisis, it is evident that many companies and investments disappeared, but some early risk-takers have become leading global firms, such as Amazon, Microsoft, Google, and Meta. While some investment evaporated, a new market based on technology was established, currently holding a market capitalization higher than most countries.

It does not seem unreasonable to envision a similar scenario to what happened in the past. When the investor frenzy and social and media hype around AI subside, products and services associated with it will emerge. Many initiatives will fail and disappear, most of them; others will persist, have a significant social impact, and could become the leading companies of the future. Despite the promising and optimistic discourse, AI is also subject to threats that could shape its development. Those investing in this technology need to be aware of potential project liquidity risks or issues related to legislation and social responsibility that could affect its progress.

The Data Protection Commission (DPC) of Ireland's decision exemplifies how the regulatory environment affects development and innovation, and its competitiveness compared to more permissive environments concerning data protection. Following its ruling, Meta announced in June 2024 that it would halt its project to train its AI models with publicly available content from Facebook and Instagram in the European Union.

Another aspect to consider in AI development is improving its efficiency concerning environmental sustainability. According to research from the University of Massachusetts, a single generative LLM model can generate 300 tons of CO_2 emissions, and another study from the University of Riverside estimated that 700,000 liters of water were consumed for cooling data centers during the training of ChatGPT-3, predicting that AI-related activities will consume between 4000 and 7000 million cubic meters by 2027 (Glavas & Inard, 2024).

1.3 How Will AI Affect Communication?

Since the emergence of ChatGPT, one of the main lines of research in the social sciences has been its study as a development tool through case studies applied to various professional fields (Goyanes & Lopezosa, 2024). The possibilities it opens up for activities related to content creation, copywriting, inspiration for creative thinking, market data analysis, and image generation have generated considerable concern and interest among companies and professionals in the media, marketing, and communication sectors in general. Among other aspects, this high level of interest is based on its potential application to existing business value chains, the possibility of new models supported by the new technology, and, significantly, how society as a whole will be affected by the promised transformation. Generative AI (genAI) heralds a rapid revolution with the promise of optimizing tasks, generating new ideas, and boosting creativity. For any creative activity, the opportunity to explore new ways of creating hyper-personalized experiences with reduced costs is highly attractive.

A dichotomy has arisen between those who see AI as an ally for improving productivity and creative inspiration and those who view it as a threat to existing business models and numerous jobs. Perhaps the greatest risk lies in less specialized and more mechanical jobs, typically held by young individuals entering the professional workforce and starting their careers with basic functions, which are part of a necessary learning process and integration into the organization's corporate culture.

1.3.1 AI and Media Journalism

Most editors and journalists view AI "as an existential threat" (Caswell, 2024). This seems understandable, given the declining trend in a necessary social activity, a media industry in crisis, and the almost widespread precarious situation of the journalism profession. The tensions currently occurring intersect with previous conflicts related to copyright and the economic exploitation of information. Professor Martin Senftleben describes generative AI systems as parasites, "only able to imitate creativity because human works have been used as training material" (Senftleben, 2023). Another risk to consider is its use in disinformation campaigns and its consequent influence on increasing public distrust.

In 2024, various agreements were made between AI-promoting companies and prestigious media brands and outlets. For example, OpenAI has partnered with News Corp, Associated Press, The Atlantic, and the historic publication Time. The quality content from their historical archives is particularly valuable for training and designing new AI models that will enable greater accuracy in their responses and improve the generated content. Meanwhile, media companies are opening a new revenue stream in their deteriorated financial accounts and seeking to incorporate new technology to create new journalistic products for their readers and reduce costs in their professional routines.

In this context, there are winners and losers among the media. The former, typically belonging to large media or publishing groups like Axel Springer or The New York Times, have invested in research and development, thanks, among other factors, to their financial and human resources and established prestige. This situation allows them to negotiate more effectively with technology platforms and companies. On the other hand, local media are in a weaker position to negotiate and will need to explore new management strategies to survive the change.

However, AI can also represent a radical shift for small and medium-sized organizations. Among other things, it allows them to gain competitiveness by using tools and technologies with accessible functionality and reduced costs. Simple language can be used to interact with AI, and results such as text and images can be obtained without the need for IT developers. This possibility is changing the mindset in newsrooms and management teams of resource-strapped media (EBU News Report, 2024).

AI has the potential to structurally strengthen the position of news organizations, provided it helps reinforce their primary mission: to offer accurate, accessible, and relevant news that allows their audiences to make informed decisions about their lives. It can contribute to improving business operations and, consequently, to sustainability, as well as to the quality of production and the way they connect with their audiences. However, the depth and speed of change will be determined by the decisions made by the multiple stakeholders involved, including media executives and professionals, technology companies, regulatory bodies, and the public.

It is understandable to envision generative AI as destined to revolutionize journalism, especially when one falls into a self-absorbed view fueled by a fully operational propaganda machine. But it is very speculative to rigorously answer the central question: What impact will AI have on the future of news and the public arena? Until its real effects on the fundamental needs of the business are assessed, it is impossible to issue and argue a rigorous judgment. Looking at the past, rather than betting on a revolution, as some Silicon Valley fundamentalists advocate, it seems more advisable to anticipate an evolution similar to the adaptation of digital technology in recent decades. It is worth remembering: "AI will not be a panacea for the many deep-seated problems and challenges facing journalism and the public arena. Technology alone cannot fix intractable political, social, and economic ills" (Simon, 2024: 39).

New uses of AI are allowing for modifications in the production of certain journalistic genres, such as reporting, and enabling previously unknown communicative possibilities. An example is the project Exhibit AI: The Refugee Account (2023), spearheaded by the Maurice Blackburn law firm, specializing in social justice, and the creative agency Howatson+Company (Maurice Blackburn, 2023). This project seeks to document the lives of survivors in Australia's offshore migrant detention centers. The refugees' own accounts reflect their experiences, and given the difficulties of filming in these locations, the images depicting this reality have been generated by AI. While it is noted that the images themselves are not real, the experiences they reflect are. The project's proponents justify their use by emphasizing the power of the stark images to expose this situation to the public and attempt to eradicate it. Just as drawing, illustration, or infographics have historically been used as visual elements of information due to technological issues or restrictions on camera access—and to enhance spectacle and public appeal—AI can now be used for similar purposes.

1.3.2 AI, Marketing, and Advertising

In the marketing and advertising sector, where novelty is one of the distinguishing features, the formulation of numerous and diverse approaches has been constant. This is due to the need for indispensable differentiation from competitors and the necessary justification of intangible and, consequently, complex proposals to evaluate from an economic perspective. While the term innovation presents some complexity in defining it precisely due to its subjectivity, the complexity increases when combined with other terms such as strategy or brand (Baraybar and Luque de Marcos, 2018).

From the results of studies and reports consulted, there seems to be a consensus among professionals regarding the significant impact that generative AI (genAI) will have in the short term on the marketing and advertising industry. It is frequently described as a disruptive technology for these organizations and their current business models. However, the use of AI in advertising over the past decades is evident, and academic interest in this field has significantly increased since 2018 (Ford et al., 2023). Its use has contributed to the production of personalized advertising by opening new avenues in understanding consumer behavior, optimizing media planning and purchasing, ad production, and impact evaluation (Chen et al., 2019; Deng et al., 2019; Li, 2019).

A report from the research and consulting firm Forrester indicates that 61% of advertising agencies in the United States have incorporated AI into their activities and 30% are exploring its use. Larger agencies are more proactive with generative AI, with 69% using it in creative agencies compared to 57% in media agencies (Forrester, 2024). Confirmation of these data would indicate a high level of acceptance in the sector compared to other fields and activities. Its application in the creative process of generating ideas or brainstorming allows for an increased number of options and faster creation and production. Among the most implemented uses in daily routines is media reporting, which enables the interpretation of audience data into insights that add value to the organization.

For example, Salesforce introduced Copilot in May 2024, which promises to enhance Customer Relationship Management (CRM). This tool can automatically generate briefs or email marketing campaigns. Thus, it allows for the automation of routine tasks and reduces time spent on project design in the data analysis phase. Additionally, the use of Microsoft Copilot, integrated into the widely used Microsoft 365 program, provides a clear advantage in presenting creative ideas to clients by facilitating content creation, image design, or music composition.

In a society where influencer marketing holds significant prominence, the ability to create virtual influencers with AI allows brands to have greater control over the message and behavior of the character, reducing the risk of potential reputational crises, as well as lowering costs and increasing customization and versatility. However, new technologies also enable human influencers to generate content more quickly, improve quality, especially in subtitling and sound, and facilitate result measurement. Only time will tell if this is a passing trend or a bubble caused by technological novelty.

Some professionals express concern about the accuracy and quality of the data influencing generative AI. The Heinz Ketchup[1] AI campaign asked people from different continents to generate images of this type of tomato sauce using Dall-E2. According to the brand, the results were very similar to the real and original Heinz Ketchup packaging. Although this may be a mere advertising argument, it demonstrates the potential relationship between AI and collective imagination. It affirms an idea already present in society but shows its limitations in proposals that drive groundbreaking new ideas or differentiating concepts with evident risks—key aspects for creative advancement.

For certain professions in the sector, it represents a serious threat, such as catalog photographers or voice actors. The speech-to-speech function has endowed AI-generated voices with the naturalness of human communication, transforming the way audiovisual content is produced (Hernández, 2024). There are numerous examples, but among them, two related fields are already researching and

[1] Campaign in: https://www.youtube.com/watch?v=LFmpVy6eGXs

incorporating AI into their production models: visual effects (VFX) and animation. Using tools like Dall-E to generate characters allows for requesting specific work naturally and in detail through smooth interaction, reducing time and budget constraints for creators distant from the budgets of major animation studios. As with other areas, prestigious VFX studios are in a favorable position to exploit and incorporate AI into their processes. This is the case with El Ranchito, a studio that has participated in productions like Game of Thrones or The Snow Society, which, using their high-resolution internal datasets, have trained AI and developed a system to generate masks automatically in scenes filmed without chroma (Guaita, 2024).

Another aspect to consider relates to the distribution of this potential audiovisual production capacity: "we still don't know what will happen with all those infinite hours of content that will start being developed in the coming years" (De la Chica, 2024). The arrival of the internet also opened new distribution methods by leveraging the interactive possibilities of the online environment and the ubiquity of viewers connected via smartphones or streaming platforms (Baraybar-Fernandez & Linares-Palomar, 2016). However, some experimented methods aimed at empowering the viewer and boosting minority content have not guaranteed the necessary return on investment for any business (Linares-Palomar & Baraybar-Fernández, 2017).

Human beings are inherently creative, and beyond Sora or other tools, the way creative work is conducted is being transformed. These tools offer new opportunities to those who master the technology by enhancing their ability to tell effective stories. It is not a battle of human against machine, but rather a competition between humans who use the machine and those who do not. For other creators and audiovisual artists experimenting with AI, they see AI applied to audiovisual media as "a tool with tremendous potential" that enables new forms of expression (López, 2024).

1.4 Conclusions

It is evident that debates around AI center on its potential social impact and attempt to create as accurate a picture as possible of how society will look after its integration. In the scientific community, there is a widely used phrase: experiments do not fail; what fails are the expectations about their results. Undoubtedly, AI, like other technological tools, will provoke changes in professional practices and societal behavior, but whether we are truly facing a revolution remains at least questionable. Doubts arise about the ability to sustain the investment necessary for its development until its proposals become profitable; about the legislation and policies—such as those related to copyright protection, privacy, and user security—that different governments will implement, which could either foster or hinder the speed of its growth or application; also, about the sustainability of the required infrastructures; but most importantly, about the training and assimilation of its uses by specialized professionals in each sector and by society at large, ultimately demonstrating the potential that AI claims to have in transforming the daily lives of citizens.

To forecast the evolution of AI with rigor, solid theoretical foundations applied to the design of future research are necessary. Among the theories most used in research on AI in advertising, two models can be particularly useful: the Technology Acceptance Model and Trust Theory. The former argues that individuals' intention to use a technology is determined by their perception of its usefulness and ease of use, both aspects influenced by various external factors such as training and support (Van den Broeck et al., 2019); on the other hand, Trust Theory highlights trust as a fundamental aspect of human relationships, built through repeated interactions that demonstrate reliability, credibility, and benevolence (Huh et al., 2020).

The evolution toward a more automated world will change existing business models and impact crucial issues such as employment. Consequently, it seems advisable to learn to coexist with this new technology and, therefore, educate in the adaptation process. The dimensions encompassed by AI are very broad, involving different technologies directed at a wide variety of applications in various fields, making it difficult to define them and make precise predictions about their development. What seems necessary is the adoption of national strategies to leverage the opportunities provided by this change. A significant example is the initiative adopted by the Singaporean government, positioned as a global leader in AI, given its status as a hub of innovation. Notable initiatives include the Infocomm Media Development Authority (IMDA) with a training program aimed at boosting worker education, and AI Singapore, which offers grants for AI research (ICEX, 2024). Additionally, there is a program for academic staff focused on content creation and exploring AI's capacity to improve education.

In Europe, legislative efforts to establish necessary ethical boundaries for technology and defend citizens' data privacy are significant, though not always aligned with the economic interests of major tech companies and investors. Data quality and transparency in its collection and interpretation are essential to avoid potential biases in the proposed models.

In summary, a vast amount of intellectual research remains to be conducted. While this may seem daunting at first, it also has a playful aspect by stimulating our imagination in the face of a new landscape with multiple possibilities. There is a need to digest this rapid change that breaks down entry barriers for the general population; interacting with technology no longer requires programming skills; verbal interaction through speech now makes it possible, breaking one of the barriers to receiving the benefits of digitization. Just as consumer behaviors evolved with the ease of access to and creation of information, new habits are likely to emerge, such as listening to messages on WhatsApp or watching videos on YouTube at double speed, or even the rise of new global languages gaining prominence, as with memes. While this happens, we must rely on critical thinking and question the notion that machines should replace humans in decision-making, avoiding the belief that AI is the new truth machine (Lie Detector) and evading any responsibility in decision-making.

References

Baraybar, A., & Luque de Marcos, J. (2018). New trends in brand building: An approach to storydoing. *Prisma Social Journal, 23*, 435–458. Retrieved from https://revistaprismasocial.es/article/view/2745

Baraybar-Fernandez, A., & Linares-Palomar, R. (2016). New proposals for audiovisual distribution in the era of convergence: the documentary book. *Profesional De La Informacion, 25*(1), 135–142. https://doi.org/10.3145/epi.2016.ene.13

Caswell, D. (2024). *How media managers think AI might transform the news ecosystem*. Reuters Institute for the Study of Journalism. https://reutersinstitute.politics.ox.ac.uk/news/how-media-managers-think-ai-might-transform-news-ecosystem

Chen, G., Xie, P., Dong, J., & Wang, T. (2019). Understanding programmatic creative: The role of AI. *Journal of Advertising, 48*(4), 347–355. https://doi.org/10.1080/00913367.2019.1654421

De la Chica, J. (2024). *Do creators dream of electric movies? The AI revolution 2024*. Ortega-Marañón Foundation. https://theairevolution.info/congreso-ai-revolution-2024-ponencias/

Deng, S., Tan, C. W., Wang, W., & Pan, Y. (2019). Smart generation system of personalized advertising copy and its application to advertising practice and research. *Journal of Advertising, 48*(4), 356–365. https://doi.org/10.1080/00913367.2019.1652121

EBU News Report. (2024). Trusted journalism in the age of generative AI. *Eurovision News*. https://www.ebu.ch/guides/open/report/news-report-2024-trusted-journalism-in-the-age-of-generative-ai

Ford, J., Jain, V., Wadhwani, K., & Gupta, D. G. (2023). AI advertising: An overview and guidelines. *Journal of Business Research, 166*, 114124. https://doi.org/10.1016/j.jbusres.2023.114124

Forrester (2024). *The state of generative AI inside US agencies*. June 14. https://www.forrester.com/report/the-state-of-generative-ai-inside-us-agencies-2024/RES180989

Glavas, D., & Inard, L. (2024). *Baromètre IA: Entreprise et Durabilité*. Institut AI for Sustainability (ESSCA).

Goyanes, M., & Lopezosa, C. (2024). ChatGPT in social sciences: A literature review on the use of OpenAI's artificial intelligence (AI) in qualitative and quantitative research. *Anuario ThinkEPI, 18*. doi:https://doi.org/10.3145/thinkepi.2024.e18a04

Guaita, D. (2024). *Applications of AI to VFX at El Ranchito. The AI Revolution 2024*. Fundación Ortega-Marañón. https://theairevolution.info/congreso-ai-revolution-2024-ponencias/

Hernández, J. (2024). *Artificial intelligence: Wave or Tsunami? The AI Revolution 2024*. Fundación Ortega-Marañón. https://theairevolution.info/congreso-ai-revolution-2024-ponencias/

Huh, J., Kim, H., Rath, B., Lu, X., & Srivastava, J. (2020). You reap where you sow: a trust-based approach to initial seeding for viral advertising. *International Journal of Advertising, 39*(7), 963–989. https://doi.org/10.1080/02650487.2020.1718823

ICEX. (2024). *Artificial Intelligence in Singapore. 20 de marzo*. https://www.icex.es/content/dam/es/icex/oficinas/113/documentos/2024/03/fichas-sector/FS_Inteligencia%20artificial%20en%20Singapur%202024_REV.pdf

Kindleberger, C. P. (2016). Bubbles in history. In G. Jones (Ed.), *Banking crises: Perspectives from the new palgrave dictionary* (pp. 37–38). Palgrave Macmillan. https://doi.org/10.1057/9781137553799_6

Li, H. (2019). Special section introduction: Artificial intelligence and advertising. *Journal of Advertising, 48*(4), 333–337. https://doi.org/10.1080/00913367.2019.1654947

Li, G., Chen, Y., Zhang, J., Li, J., Guo, S., & Zhang, T. (2024). *Warfare: Breaking the watermark protection of AI-Generated Content*. Preprint at. https://doi.org/10.48550/arXiv.2310.07726.

Linares-Palomar, R., & Baraybar-Fernández, A. (2017). The empowerment of the film spectators: Theatrical on demand in Spain. *Profesional De La información, 26*(1), 67–76. https://doi.org/10.3145/epi.2017.ene.07

López, A. G. (2024). *Is AI an artistic medium? The AI revolution 2024*. Fundación Ortega-Marañón. https://theairevolution.info/congreso-ai-revolution-2024-ponencias/

López-García, X. (2024). ReImagining intelligent journalism. *Anuario ThinkEPI, 18*, e18e02. https://doi.org/10.3145/thinkepi.2024.e18a02

Maurice Blackburn. (2023). *Exhibit AI: The refugee account*. https://www.exhibitai.com.au/
Metz, C., Weise, K. Grant, N. & Isaac, M. (2023). Ego, fear and money: How the AI fuse was lit. *The New York Times*. December, 3. https://www.nytimes.com/2023/12/03/technology/ai-openai-musk-page-altman.html (consultado 05/07/2024).
Park, P. S., Goldstein, S., O'Gara, A., Chen, M., & Hendrycks, D. (2024). AI deception: A survey of examples, risks, and potential solutions. *Patterns, 5*(5). https://doi.org/10.1016/j.patter.2024.100988
Piglia, R. (2011). *Los usos de la narración. En Hirschman, S. Gente y cuentos ¿A quién pertenece la literatura? Las comunidades encuentran su voz a través de los cuentos*. Fondo de Cultura Económica.
Popper, K. R. (1974). Replies to my critics. In P. A. Schilpp (Ed.), *The philosophy of Karl Popper, vol. XIV of The library of living philosophers* (pp. 961–1197). Open Court. Book II.
Price Waterhouse Coopers. (2024). *Global workforce hopes and fears survey 2024*. PwC, June 24. https://www.pwc.es/es/consultoria/consultoria-people-organisation/hopes-and-fears-2024.html (consultado 13/07/2024).
Quinn, W., & Turner, J. D. (2020). Bubbles in history. *Business History, 65*(4), 636–655. https://doi.org/10.1080/00076791.2020.1844668
Senftleben, M. (2023). Generative AI and author remuneration. *International Review of Intellectual Property and Competition Law, 54*, 1535–1560. https://doi.org/10.2139/ssrn.4478370
Shah, C., & Bender, E. M. (2024). Envisioning information access systems: What makes for good tools and a healthy Web? *ACM Transactions on the Web, 18*(3), 1–24. https://doi.org/10.1145/3649468
Sheikh, H., Prins, C., & Schrijvers, E. (2023). AI as a system technology. In *Mission AI. Research for policy*. Springer. https://doi.org/10.1007/978-3-031-21448-6_4
Siegel, J. J. (2003). What is an asset price bubble? An operational definition. *European Financial Management, 9*(1), 11–24. https://doi.org/10.1111/1468-036X.00206
Simon, F. (2024). *Artificial intelligence in the news: How AI retools, rationalizes, and reshapes journalism and the public arena*. Tow Center for Digital Journalism, Columbia University. https://ora.ox.ac.uk/objects/uuid:aeb25013-1d17-40b2-b471-5bdca309db87
Van den Broeck, E., Zarouali, B., & Poels, K. (2019). Chatbot advertising effectiveness: When does the message get through? *Computers in Human Behavior, 98*, 150–157. https://doi.org/10.1016/j.chb.2019.04.009

Antonio Baraybar-Fernández, Full Professor of Audiovisual Communication and Advertising at the Rey Juan Carlos University. Ph.D. in Information Sciences from the Complutense University of Madrid. Member of the high-performance research group at URJC: INFOCENT. His research interests are related to Communication Economics, Communication Management in Organizations, and Neuroscience applied to Communication. He has published his studies and research in prestigious international and Spanish publishing houses, as well as in academic journals indexed in the world's leading databases. He has served as the Vice-Dean of Technology and Resources for the Faculty of Communication Sciences and as the head of the Department of Communication and Sociology Sciences at URJC. He has also been the director of the Francisco Villamartín chair (CESEDEN-URJC).

Sandro Arrufat-Martín, Cum Laude Doctor in Communication Sciences from the Rey Juan Carlos University (2021). Master in Protocol, Communication and Comprehensive Organization of Events from the URJC (2018) and Master in Corporate Communication Management from EAE Business School (2017). Bachelor's Degree in Journalism from UDIMA (2016). Currently, associate professor at the Rey Juan Carlos University, having won a competitive contest in the Department of Audiovisual Communication and Advertising. He teaches at both undergraduate and master's levels at the International University of La Rioja (UNIR), EAE Business School and the Madrid Chamber of Commerce. In addition, he is the author of journals indexed in the Arts & Humanities

Citation Index (A&HCI) of Web of Science, Scopus, Emerging Sources Citation Index (ESCI), Latindex, among others. He has also published book chapters included in Scholarly Publishers Indicators (SPI). In addition, he has been involved in various research projects related to digital communication management and strategies, social networks and corporate reputation. Likewise, his research areas include public relations, branding and corporate communication.

Chapter 2
OpenAI and Bain & Company: A Strategic Alliance to Optimize Technology and Its Applicability

Marina Rodríguez Hernández, Isabel A. Vázquez Sacristán, and Miguel Baños González

2.1 Introduction

Artificial intelligence (AI) has evolved significantly since its inception, transforming from a mere theoretical conceptualization to an integral tool in various areas, including communication (Conde & Núñez, 2023). From the creation of the first algorithms to advances in deep learning and neural networks, AI has enabled the development of systems capable of performing complex tasks that previously required human intervention (Russell & Norvig, 2020). AI, defined as the ability of a machine to mimic human intelligence through algorithms and mathematical models (Nilsson, 1982), has been adopted in multiple sectors, with communication being one of the fields that has experienced the greatest changes and benefits.

In terms of evolution, the first efforts in AI focused on solving specific problems through problem-solving programs and games (McCarthy et al., 2006). However, the development of machine learning techniques and advances in computational processing power have enabled the creation of more sophisticated and autonomous systems. Deep learning, a sub-discipline of machine learning that uses multi-layered artificial neural networks, has been particularly revolutionary, facilitating improved

M. R. Hernández (✉)
TBWA, Madrid, Spain
e-mail: marina.rodriguez@tbwa.com

I. A. Vázquez Sacristán
Advertising, Ideation and Brand Communication, Francisco de Vitoria University, Madrid, Spain
e-mail: isabel.vazquez@ufv.es

M. B. González
Department of Communication and Sociology, King Juan Carlos University, Móstoles, Spain
e-mail: miguel.banos@urjc.es

A. Baraybar-Fernández et al. (eds.), *The AI Revolution*, Research Series on Responsible Enterprise Ecosystems, https://doi.org/10.1007/978-3-031-80411-3_2

natural language processing (NLP) and understanding of complex contexts (LeCun et al., 2015).

In the field of communication, AI has become an essential tool for the management and analysis of large volumes of data, content personalization, and process automation. Matz et al. (2024) highlight that one of the most commonly used strategies is to match the content of the message with the psychological profile of the receiver to achieve communication effectiveness, and demonstrate, with their research, that major advances in tools such as ChatGPT, with its potential to automate processes, could expand the use of personalized persuasion and, therefore, the effectiveness of this type of messages. In a similar vein, Gupta et al. (2024) conduct a study on the use of ChatGPT in marketing, analyzing how it "may allow for more personalized and engaging content, better customer experience, and improved ROI" (p. 1), concluding that "ChatGPT has great potential as a marketing tool. Companies that leverage this technology have significant advantages over competitors" (p. 13).

AI-based tools, such as chatbots and virtual assistants, have improved the efficiency and effectiveness of interactions between businesses and customers, providing fast and accurate responses to queries and enhancing the user experience (Huang & Rust, 2018). In addition, AI is used to analyze sentiment and trends in social networks, allowing organizations to adjust their communication strategies in a more informed and real-time manner (Cambria et al., 2013).

More specifically, in the field of marketing communications, Rodgers (2021), in an article entitled "Promises and Perils of Artificial Intelligence and Advertising," considered that "Of all the technological advances in advertising, none are perhaps more exciting than artificial intelligence (AI)" (p. 1); and, despite the doubts and questions, even of an ethical nature, that arise around AI, the reality is that it promises to change "the very nature of advertising," and the changes will be perceived in all phases and stages of the advertising process. For Huh et al. (2023) advertisers are already using AI to: segment the market, develop and personalize creativity, improve the purchase of ad space, etc.; and they identify four areas that AI is substantially modifying that "open opportunities and need for research: (1) consumers' experience of advertising; (2) societal and policy implications related to the truthfulness of AI-generated content; (3) the analytical considerations of data and algorithms; and (4) the functioning of the advertising industry" (p. 478).

One of the most recent and notable advances in AI is the ability to create images from textual descriptions, known as prompts. This technology, exemplified by developments such as DALL-E or OpenAI's SORA (Flores-Vivar, 2024), allows the generation of high-quality images that correspond to a detailed description, which has significant applications in content creation and visual communication. They use deep learning models to understand and generate coherent and creative content from textual inputs (Ramesh et al., 2021). These advances not only demonstrate the power of AI in artistic creation and design, but also expand the possibilities for personalization and creativity in digital communication. In relation to this topic, Chaisatitkul et al. (2024) conducted a research to analyze the perceptions and attitudes of a sample of subjects (target audience of brands, marketing experts, and advertising professionals) toward AI-created advertising messages, showing that all three groups had a positive attitude toward AI-created works, while the target audience of brands, moreover, showed their preference for these messages.

The ongoing evolution and advances in AI promise to continue to transform communication, offering new opportunities and challenges. And the pace at which it is evolving is faster than any other advance; Chow (2023) highlights that the AI chatbot ChatGPT has reached 100 million monthly active users in just 2 months, a figure that, for example, took Instagram two and a half years to reach and TikTok 9 months. And this growth has served as an incentive for large technology companies to accelerate the development and launch of their own applications, which will totally transform advertising management and research (Huh et al., 2023).

The ability of machines to learn and adapt to new information continues to push the boundaries of what is possible, leading the way to an era in which artificial intelligence and communication are intrinsically interconnected. In this context, AI applications are revolutionizing how brands communicate with their audiences, enabling more personalized and effective interaction. Brands can now analyze large volumes of data to better understand their audiences and adapt their messages in real time, significantly improving their customer relationships and brand perception (Kaplan & Haenlein, 2019). AI's ability to generate relevant and engaging content from textual prompts appears to be facilitating the creation of campaigns that reinforce the emotional connection between brands and their audiences. Given its possibilities, some consulting firms have embarked on the development of specialized services to advise their clients on the applicability of AI in business contexts, helping organizations to implement these technologies strategically and effectively to optimize their operations and communications (Bain & Company, 2023).

2.2 The OpenAI and Bain & Co Partnership

In light of the above, in today's technological landscape, AI is emerging as a fundamental tool for business transformation and growth. Its potential to automate tasks, optimize processes, and generate new business opportunities is increasingly recognized. However, the complexity of AI and the challenges associated with its effective implementation can hinder its widespread adoption. In this context, the strategic alliance between OpenAI—a leader in AI research and development—and Bain & Company—a renowned global consulting firm—is a significant milestone in driving business adoption of AI. This collaboration brings together the experience and expertise of both parties to offer companies comprehensive solutions that enable them to take full advantage of AI's potential.

According to the communications made jointly by both entities, the main objectives of this alliance are identified as follows:

- The democratization of access to AI, as it seeks to facilitate the integration of this technology for companies of all sizes and industries, through the creation of customized solutions that adapt to the specific needs of each organization.

- Accelerating innovation, as it seeks to drive the development of new applications and use cases of AI developed by OpenAI in the business environment through Bain & Co′s strategic consulting.
- Strengthening the responsible use of AI, since one of the key points of the agreement lies in the commitment of both companies to promote the ethical use of this technology through the establishment of reference frameworks and protocols that guarantee transparency and security in the development and implementation of these AI solutions.

On the other hand, the benefits for companies that decide to take advantage of this partnership are:

- Greater efficiency and productivity, resulting from the automation of repetitive tasks that free up time for human teams to focus on performing activities that provide greater added value.
- More informed decision making, thanks to the analysis of large volumes of data by AI, leading to better market understanding, resource optimization, and greater competitive advantage.
- The creation of innovative products and services that meet changing consumer needs.
- Improved customer satisfaction and loyalty by leveraging the experience personalization capabilities offered by AI leading to more efficient, faster, and more effective services.

Given the potential impact and benefits outlined above, it is clear that the strategic implementation of AI can profoundly transform business operations. As an example, the following is an analysis of the first collaborative project resulting from this partnership: Create Real Magic for The Coca-Cola Company. To this end, data published in the case presented by the company at the Cannes Lions International Festival of Creativity will be presented, as well as information provided by the current EU Shopper Creative Lead for Coca-Cola at WPP, Daniel Pownall, in an interview conducted specifically for this research.

2.3 Study of The Coca-Cola Company's Create Real Magic project

The Coca-Cola Company's Create Real Magic is a benchmark for the application of AI in the consumer goods sector. It was announced and implemented at the end of March 2023, shortly after the signing of the agreement between OpenAI and Bain & Co. To facilitate its use, on March 21, 2023, Coca-Cola launched an explanatory video on how to participate, which can be consulted through the following link: https://www.youtube.com/watch?v=FPGDMj1QUBE

«While some brands and people choose to fight AI technology, Coca-Cola is choosing to embrace it» (Cannes Lions, 2023) (see Fig. 2.1). As described in the file included on the website of the aforementioned International Festival of Creativity:

> The objective was simple: show how Coca-Cola is an early adopter of AI, and engage the creative community in an unexpected way that shows the potential that generative AI and endless human imagination can have when brought together—in a way that only Coca-Cola can do. To democratize AI and make it more approachable, Coca-Cola invited everyone to "Create Real Magic" to celebrate the power of creativity.
>
> And they did it by handing over some of its most iconic assets that have lived in culture for decades for artists all over the world to re-imagine using a first-of-its-kind AI platform.
>
> Leveraging hundreds of images as their canvas—such as the distinctive Coca-Cola bottle, polar bears, and Santa Claus—Coca-Cola invited artists to co-create original artwork to show the possibilities of using generative AI to create art.

To incentivize participation, the brand offered two rewards: (1) the display of the best works on iconic billboards in Times Square and Piccadilly Circus and (2) to be one of thirty artists invited to the Real Magic Creative Academy, a 3-day workshop that facilitated a meeting between these global creators and Coca-Cola Atlanta's in-house design team.

For all of this, a web platform was created that made DALL-E and GPT's generative AI accessible to all Internet users for the first time, allowing anyone to experiment with the technology and create original works of art from some of the soft drink brand's most iconic images, such as the contour bottle or its famous polar bears.

Fig. 2.1 Image of the case published in "The Work" section of Cannes Lions. Source: https://www.lovethework.com/work-awards/campaigns/create-real-magic-ai-1529622

After 2 weeks in a selection of countries, more than 120,000 new images around Coca-Cola were obtained as can be seen in these publications made by the firm on Instagram, both in its global profile—https://www.instagram.com/p/CqBlBM-hAxP/—and UK—https://www.instagram.com/p/CqlEA2KIhPh/-. Excluding paid media, the campaign generated more than five thousand posts on the networks, obtained an organic social reach of more than 300 million impressions, a positive sentiment of 90% and great media coverage in more than 20 countries.

In addition, at Christmas, the platform was reinstated as part of the global campaign "The World Need more Santas." In fact, the content currently available on the website www.createrealmagic.com is related to this latest brand activation (see Fig. 2.2).

According to the statements made by Pownall (2024), this Christmas campaign has been decisive for Coca-Cola because it has allowed it to recover the notoriety and relevance it had years ago. In line with what has been published by different specialized advertising media, he comments that it has been a campaign in which generative artificial intelligence has been remarkably integrated, empowering users and turning them into "viralizers" of Christmas, hand in hand with Coca-Cola. In this regard, he expresses the interest of the soft drink brand in integrating itself into popular culture and how, in this case, it has done so by making its most symbolic assets available to the general public so that they can "play" with them.

The interviewee highlights the brand's collaboration with various companies to develop their own artificial intelligence tools, which reflects a comprehensive strategy that encompasses all business processes. Significantly, he emphasizes that this

Fig. 2.2 Collage of images posted on www.createrealmagic.com with Christmas theme. Source: https://www.createrealmagic.com/

technology is intended to be integrated at all levels of the company, as it is considered a very helpful auxiliary tool. In this sense, all the briefs given by the brand for some time now include the request to explore the application of these technologies to generate leads and foster the community of users around the company, which suggests a strategic vision that seeks to maximize the value of AI in the advertising and creative context.

The interview inevitably brings up the debate on the current landscape of advertising, design, and communication as it relates to Artificial Intelligence and the impact on employment and creativity within the industry. Some experts argue that AI represents a threat that could destroy jobs and homogenize creative output. However, Daniel Pownall offers an alternative perspective, based on his practical experience, in which AI is presented as a powerful tool that expands creative possibilities and facilitates project execution. Pownall argues that, rather than fearing AI, we should focus on understanding it and harnessing its capabilities to enhance our work. AI allows us to explore ideas and concepts that were previously unimaginable to clients, while streamlining and optimizing previously time-consuming processes.

We also extract as relevant information, what the interviewee said about generation Z. Brands such as Coca-Cola are focused on this target audience, being these users the main drivers of this type of innovative actions by brands. This generation of users is characterized by valuing co-creation, differentiation, and the feeling of belonging, which is reflected in their participation in this type of initiatives. That is why currently all the strategies of large companies focus on generating actions in which AI has a significant presence.

Finally, the brand has identified the need to implement innovative actions in regions such as Eastern Europe, where competition is more intense and closer to the Z generation. In this context, the brand has decided to focus on artificial intelligence as a key tool to connect with the new generations, reflecting an adaptive and proactive strategy in this environment and in the advertising actions being considered.

2.4 Conclusion

The importance of co-creation for new generations and the pursuit of viralization through user-generated content is leading brands to be less strict with their corporate visual identity elements than they were in the past. However, this does not mean that they are not zealously watching over the proper professional use of their identity assets. However, they have understood that the iconic elements that build their personality have transcended corporate control, have become part of popular culture and that, consequently, users feel comfortable participating in their transformation and, beyond that, they want to share their interventions.

In line with the findings derived from the interview with Daniel Pownall, it is inferred that similar actions are viable and can achieve satisfactory results in renowned brands such as Coca-Cola, since their visual elements are sufficiently recognizable to generate a representative impact. The iconicity of brands such as the one investigated implies the existence of a cultural footprint that allows users to get involved, enjoy the proposed activities and make them feel part of the actions of these corporations. The involvement of brands with high levels of acceptance by consumers, which promote the creation of organic content through their communities of affine, means that these tools offer new opportunities for connection and relationship. This type of creative actions, in which consumers are the creators of a large part of the content, encourage them to spread and expand the idea by feeling directly involved in the communication campaign. Therefore, proposals in which the user assumes a leading role in the final result and can feel identified with the outcome are essential for iconic brands such as Coca-Cola, which seek to establish an effective connection with these new audiences. Generation Z, defined by its familiarity with technology and its search for personalized experiences, represents a key segment in current marketing strategies. These actions of co-creation and proactive user participation allow companies to generate a closer and more meaningful bond with this demographic group, fostering a sense of belonging and differentiation that is crucial in a highly competitive environment.

On the other hand, thanks to the conversation held, it has been noted that the integration of AI tools in daily creative work processes is starting to become a reality. They streamline processes and optimize the use of human resources, especially in the sketching and idea presentation phases. In this sense, AI is not presented as a replacement for human creativity, but as an ally that complements and enriches it. By embracing the possibilities offered by AI, industry professionals can raise their level of work and deliver innovative and differentiating results. Pownall and Coca-Cola's stance invites a change in thinking about the relationship between AI and the creative sector. Instead of seeing it as a threat, it should be embraced as a tool that opens new doors to expression and communication, allowing industry professionals to leverage their talent and offer added value to their clients.

Innovation in advertising creation processes is one of the areas positively affected by the inclusion of these tools, as AI allows advertisers to analyze large sets of customer data—such as their online behavior, preferences, trends, and many other details—to create personalized and highly targeted advertising campaigns. This translates into more relevant and engaging messages for each individual, increasing the chances of conversion and loyalty.

On the other hand, the creation of public AI platforms serves to test the use of the technology on a large scale, improving its learning and, therefore, its results. For this reason, the agreement between OpenAI and Bain & Co is particularly interesting, as it combines OpenAI's technical expertise with Bain & Co's strategic consulting, boosting the effective implementation of AI solutions through the involvement of entities that already have a high level of social acceptance in the markets. Thus, the interactions that are promoted generate a huge amount of data, which are essential for continuous learning and improvement of these systems. Consequently, as a result of these interventions, some particularly noteworthy advantages are identified: (1) the attainment of a wide variety of data from diverse contexts that help train more robust and generalizable models, (2) the identification of errors or limitations in the models, so that developers can make continuous adjustments and improvements to refine them, and (3) the promotion of AI adoption among the general public so that all types of users become familiar with the technology and explore its potential applications.

References

Bain & Company. (2023). *OpenAI x Bain&Company alliance.* https://www.bain.com/vector-digital/partnerships-alliance-ecosystem/openai-alliance/

Cambria, E., Schuller, B., Xia, Y., & Havasi, C. (2013). New avenues in opinion mining and sentiment analysis. *IEEE Intelligent Systems, 28*(2), 15–21. https://doi.org/10.1109/MIS.2013.30

Cannes Lions. (2023). *Create real magic AI.* https://www.lovethework.com/work-awards/campaigns/create-real-magic-ai-1529622

Chaisatitkul, A., Luangngamkhum, K., Noulpum, K., et al. (2024). The power of AI in marketing: enhancing efficiency and improving customer perception through AI-generated storyboards. *International Journal of Information Technology, 16*, 137–144. https://doi.org/10.1007/s41870-023-01661-5

Chow, A. R. (February 8, 2023). How ChatGPT managed to grow faster than TikTok or Instagram? *Time*. https://time.com/6253615/chatgpt-fastest-growing/

Conde, P. & Núñez, J. A. (December 18, 2023). La Revolución del Pensamiento Digital: La Evolución de la Inteligencia Artificial y los Modelos de Lenguaje. *EY España.* https://www.ey.com/es_es/the-cfo-agenda/la-revolucion-pensamiento-digital-la-evolucion-inteligencia-artifical-los-modelos-lenguaje

Flores-Vivar, J. (February 20, 2024). *SORA, un hito en la evolución de la inteligencia artificial con impacto en los medios y otras industrias.* Madri+d Blog Cultura de red. https://www.madrimasd.org/blogs/culturadered/sora-un-hito-en-la-evolucion-de-la-inteligencia-artificial-con-impacto-en-los-medios-y-otras-industrias/

Gupta, R., Nair, K., Mishra, M., Ibrahim, B., & Bhardwaj, S. (2024). Adoption and impacts of generative artificial intelligence: Theoretical underpinnings and research agenda. *International Journal of Information Management Data Insights, 4*(1), 1–15. 100232. doi:https://doi.org/10.1016/j.jjimei.2024.100232.

Huang, M.-H., & Rust, R. T. (2018). Artificial intelligence in service. *Journal of Service Research, 21*(2), 155–172. https://doi.org/10.1177/1094670517752459

Huh, J., Nelson, M. R., & Russell, C. A. (2023). ChatGPT, AI advertising, and advertising research and education. *Journal of Advertising, 52*(4), 477–482. https://doi.org/10.1080/00913367.2023.2227013

Kaplan, A., & Haenlein, M. (2019). Siri, Siri, in my hand: Who's the fairest in the land? On the interpretations, illustrations and implications of artificial intelligence. *Business Horizons, 62*(1), 15–25. https://doi.org/10.1016/j.bushor.2018.08.004

LeCun, Y., Bengio, Y., & Hinton, G. (2015). Deep learning. *Nature, 521*, 43–444. https://doi.org/10.1038/nature14539

Matz, S. C., Teeny, J. D., Vaid, S. S., et al. (2024). The potential of generative AI for personalized persuasion at scale. *Scientific Reports, 14*, 4692. (2024). https://doi.org/10.1038/s41598-024-53755-0

McCarthy, J., Minsky, M. L., Rochester, N. & Shannon, C. E. (2006). A proposal for the Dartmouth Summer Research Project on Artificial Intelligence, August 31, 1955. *AI Magazine*, 27(4), 12, pp. 12–14. doi:https://doi.org/10.1609/aimag.v27i4.1904.

Nilsson, N. J. (1982). *Principles of artificial intelligence*. Springer.

Ramesh, A., Pavlov, M., Goh, G., Gray, S., Voss, C., Radford, A., Chen, M., & Sutskever, I. (2021). Zero-shot text-to-image generation. *Cornell University ArXiv, 2102*, 12092. https://doi.org/10.48550/arXiv.2102.12092

Rodgers, S. (2021). Themed issue introduction: promises and perils of artificial intelligence and advertising. *Journal of Advertising, 50*(1), 1–10. https://doi.org/10.1080/00913367.2020.1868233

Russell, S., & Norvig, P. (2020). *Artificial intelligence: A modern approach* (4th ed.). Pearson.

Marina Rodríguez Hernández, PhD in Communication from King Juan Carlos University of Madrid. Senior Art Director at the multinational advertising agency TBWA. Academic Director of the Master in Fashion, Beauty and Luxury Branding at Francisco de Vitoria University. She has been assistant professor at the Department of Communication and Sociology at King Juan Carlos University of Madrid, teaching subjects related to corporate communication. Previously, she was a professor of the Degree in Advertising at the Francisco de Vitoria University for 14 years, teaching subjects such as Merchandising Techniques, Network Marketing, Design Tools, Campaign Production or Advertising Law. As a result of his research activity, she has published articles in different journals indexed in selective databases such as Scopus. She has also published about 20 book chapters and has been co-editor of a book. Her lines of research address Branding and the application of New Technologies in Advertising and Communication of FMCG and Luxury Brands.

Isabel A. Vázquez Sacristán, Director of the Degree in Advertising, Ideation and Brand Communication at the Francisco de Vitoria University. She has been teaching for more than 8 years focused on the area of Advertising Creativity and Campaigning. Nominated for best University Professor in Spain by the EducaAbanca platform in the 23/24 academic year. Her lines of research are based on the adoption of New Technologies by Brands for the creation of Campaigns and Experiential actions. As a result of his research activity, she has published articles in different journals indexed in selective databases such as Scopus. She has also published about twenty book chapters and has been co-editor of a book. She has more than 10 years of professional experience as account manager in national and international advertising agencies managing clients such as Pullmantur, Grupo Schweppes, Swatch, Grupo Mahou San Miguel, LFP, Telefónica, and Aegon Assurance, among others. Her experience in the industry has allowed her to develop a deep understanding of current trends and challenges in the world of advertising and bring them to the classroom and research.

Miguel Baños González, PhD in Information Sciences from the Complutense University of Madrid. University Professor in the area of Audiovisual Communication and Advertising, at King Juan Carlos University of Madrid, since 2006, teaching subjects of creativity, copywriting and advertising planning. From March 2018 to March 2022 he has been Dean of the Faculty of Communication Sciences at King Juan Carlos University. He has extensive research experience, having participated in various research projects, funded in public calls, national and international (European Commission; European Regional Development Fund, Community of Madrid; Ministry of Economy, Industry and Competitiveness; Ministry of Education, Culture and Sport; Ministry of Foreign Affairs; etc.). Within his research activity he is a member of the consolidated research group in Communication and Digital Culture of the Universidad Rey Juan Carlos (Ciberimaginario) and of the High-Performance Research Group in the Communication of Social Causes of the Universidad Rey Juan Carlos (SIC). He is also a member of the scientific association Icono14. As a result of his research activity, he has published articles in different national and international journals, indexed in selective databases such as JCR or Scopus. He has also published 8 books and more than 20 book chapters. Since 2017 he has published different articles, book chapters and has been co-editor of a book focused on the field of Neuromarketing. His lines of research address

Neuromarketing, Scientific Communication, Social Advertising, New Technologies, Marketing Communication Tools and Advertising Creativity. He has also developed an extensive professional activity as copywriter or creative director, from 1986 to 2004, in different national and international advertising agencies.

Chapter 3
Ethical Considerations in the Use of Artificial Intelligence in the Audiovisual Field

Rebeca-Illiana Arévalo-Martínez, Rogelio Del Prado Flores, and Ricardo Ignacio Prado-Hurtado

3.1 Introduction

The relevance that Artificial Intelligence (AI) has gained in recent years on a global level was unimaginable when it emerged more than 70 years ago. The applications of AI in its first decades were mainly limited to the field of computing and engineering. Research on AI has increased exponentially in recent years. Between 2013 and 2022, the articles published worldwide on the topic have been mainly in sciences such as computing (65%), engineering (38%), and mathematics (21%). However, in social sciences it barely reaches 6% (Barrere et al., 2023), hence the importance of continuing to contribute to research in this case in the field of communication, particularly in the audiovisual one.

The objective of this chapter is to present the origins and evolution of artificial intelligence, the development of AI in the audiovisual industry, and the revolution of AI in the audiovisual field and human safety, to conclude with the proposal of ethical considerations of the use of AI in the audiovisual field.

This chapter details the main contributions of AI within the audiovisual industry for more than 30 years and the reasons why there are complaints from unions that have been affected by not being informed about its use, putting their laboral future at risk. On the other hand, it presents the applications of AI in the audiovisual field applied to car driving, which have been very relevant for human safety, mobility, and environmental care.

Finally, the contributions of international organizations on the ethics of artificial intelligence are presented and different theoretical elements are provided that

R.-I. Arévalo-Martínez (✉) · R. D. P. Flores · R. I. Prado-Hurtado
Centro de Investigación para la Comunicación Aplicada, Facultad de Comunicación, Universidad Anáhuac México, Huixquilucan, Mexico
e-mail: rebeca.arevalo@anahuac.mx; rogelio.delprado2@anahuac.mx; r.prado@anahuac.mx

A. Baraybar-Fernández et al. (eds.), *The AI Revolution*, Research Series on Responsible Enterprise Ecosystems, https://doi.org/10.1007/978-3-031-80411-3_3

support the reflection on the relevance and unique value of the human being in the creation of the social link as a fundamental element to achieve the common good, and the respect for human rights based on the truth.

3.2 Origins and Evolution of Artificial Intelligence

The origins of artificial intelligence are more than 70 years ago. In 1950 Alan Turing created the test that bears his surname and evaluates the ability of machines to impersonate humans. In 1956 John McCarthy coined the term artificial intelligence. While in 1957 Frank Rosenblat designed what is considered the first artificial neural network and in 1966 the first computer communication with human language (first chatbot) was carried out (National Geographic España, 2025).

The development since then has not stopped. The applications and updates that artificial intelligence has had are many. Philip Boucher (2020) in his report Artificial Intelligence: How does it work? Because it is important? And what can we do about it? presented in the European Parliament establishes three waves or generations of AI: (1) capable of following instructions in a system of simple pre-established rules; (2) equipped with machine learning that learns and allows complex proposals to be developed through the use of enormous databases that lead to decision-making (Generative AI); and (3) able to interpret context, design solutions to new problems, and develop consciousness (Ciucci & Gouardères, 2020).

Artificial intelligence is composed of many technologies such as machine learning, neural networks, deep learning, natural language processing, computer vision, data science, and robotics (Red de Indicadores de Ciencia y Tecnología Iberoamericana e Interamericana [RICYT], 2023). Among the properties of artificial intelligence, transparency (questioning it about its own functioning) and honesty (reliability of its predictions) stand out, which allows the existence of applications such as visual recognition, natural language recognition, strategy and planning, diagnosis, support in decision-making, and human–computer collaboration (Foro Consultivo Científico y Tecnológico, 2018).

AI has evolved exponentially in recent years with the development of more specialized algorithms, with a greater amount of data available and greater human and financial resources. Currently, artificial intelligence can be defined as "it's a machine that can learn things we don't know and can make decisions independently and can create completely new ideas that no human being have ever thought about" (Harari, 2024, 15m11s). In this sense, there are various concerns about the scope of AI in the coming years.

> About the regulation of AI is first of all to make sure that the AI remains accountable and understandable. If we reach a point when we can no longer understand it, then at least in democratic societies is the end of democracy (Harari, 2024, 20m44s).

While it is true, the applications and advances that AI allows in various aspects of human life are important and have positive impacts. There is also the possibility that the applications generated by artificial intelligence, not being understood by humans, generate problems that are difficult to solve without artificial intelligence. This is why there must be ethical criteria and respect for regulation on the increasingly growing topic worldwide.

3.3 Artificial Intelligence in the Audiovisual Industry

Artificial Intelligence (AI) as a topic in the audiovisual industry dates back to 1968 with the film titled "2001: A Space Odyssey," and from then on, it has been featured in a series of movies and series with AI as a central theme—often exploring AI gaining self-awareness and unleashing dystopian futures: Westworld (1973, 2016), Blade Runer (1982, 2017), Terminator (1984, 1991, 2003, 2009, 2015, 2019), Matrix (1999), Minority Report (2002), WALL-E (2008), Ex Machina (2014), among many others (Batlle, 2023). Based on these narratives, it can be considered that the public perception of AI is not entirely favorable (Rey, 2023). Perhaps for this reason, the current encounter of humanity with an exponentially growing AI generates certain apprehensions (Rey, 2023).

However, the first use of AI in the audiovisual industry, specifically in cinema, was in 1993 with the use of computer-generated images (CGI) in the film Jurassic Park through the rendering engine called RenderMan from Pixar (Europa Press, 2015). Today the use of AI in the audiovisual industry is a reality that has different scopes. To create visual effects, computer vision (Vilaça et al., 2020), deep learning (Nawaz et al., 2023), or content generation (Cádiz, 2020) are used. Machine learning is used to create content (Wang et al., 2023). Natural Language Processing is used to generate scripts (Bazán-Gil, 2023; Cádiz, 2020). And for the streaming services, content personalization is used (Nevsky, 2023)—to mention some of the most used technologies.

First, AI makes it possible to improve the reproduction of audiovisual environments or contexts that would not be physically possible to recreate or that would have a high production cost. However, on the second place, there is the possibility that production companies reproduce the image and voice of their actors without their consent through the so-called Generative Artificial Intelligence (Generative AI). This technology has put AI in the eye of the storm, as it has also presented itself as the entry tool for ordinary people into the audiovisual industry (Madiega, 2019). Additionally, the development of neural networks trained from machine learning has allowed AI to imitate human learning processes (Penrose, 2016; Searle, 2023). This fact has generated an unprecedented development in Generative AI tools such as text, image and animation processors, voice processors, and audiovisual content with a practically unimaginable future projection (Searle, 2015, 2023). The greatest investments, advances, and applications of the Generative AI in the audiovisual industry have been made in the most profitable activities such as cinema, advertising, video journalism, or pornography (San Juan, 2023). It seems that the current trend is the appropriation of technologies and experimentation with them in almost all aspects of life, not only in the commercial and professional realms, but also in the personal and intimate ones (Prado-Hurtado, 2022).

The applications of Generative AI have occurred at the three levels of audiovisual production: pre-production, production, and post-production (Hinojosa Becerra et al., 2024). In pre-production, data from millions of people who consciously or involuntarily provide fundamental data for creative decision-making are mathematically and statistically crossed (Batlle, 2023). In this case we find the magical algorithm like the thinking machine (Turing, 1905). Originally it was about processing big data to guarantee the success (Aguilar, 2013) of the first series that Netflix developed for exclusive streaming: House of Cards. This political drama had all the innovative production elements, thanks to technology, in addition to the growing taste for series marathons (Ramírez, 2018). This algorithm, today supported by Generative AI, designs most of the content, accelerating and systematizing the process, providing more and better Key Performance Indicators (KPI) to support decisions (Netflix, 2024).

In the production process, content generated by Generative AI is used to credibly present extraordinary effects in which talents can be generated, rejuvenated, or even revived, with all the ethical implications that this entails (Bazán-Gil, 2023). An example is a recent advertising campaign by Volkswagen Brazil, where the famous singers Maria Rita and Elis Regina, daughter and mother, respectively, sing a duet of the song Como Nossos Pais with the particularity that Regina died 42 years before launching the campaign (Volkswagen do Brasil, 2023). In the field of audiovisual production, the possibilities have become infinite, new tools are launched every day that make processes simpler and with better results (Bordignon et al., 2023).

In the post-production phase, the Generative AI can develop virtually any visual environment that can be requested through detailed instructions (prompts). The environments are carefully designed, and it is possible to modify or reinterpret them in an extraordinarily realistic way (Bazán-Gil, 2023). Currently, the biggest challenge is the design of prompts to guarantee the digital values of post-production and not the use of technologies that apparently have no limits (Vilaça et al., 2020).

Among the AI applications that are currently considered standard is the digital facial overlay or deepfake. The tool that has democratized the production of deepfakes is Vidnoz (2024) with a result superior to many other platforms, since it does not require a database of images of the person to be impersonated and is free. In terms of sound, a tool that has achieved superior results is ElevenLabs (2024), since it allows you to modulate the voice and intonation until the cloning is perfect, overtaking the popular HeyGen (2024) for being more accessible. For the artificial generation of videos, the current standard is SORA from the giant OpenAI with results that really deceive the eye (OpenAI, 2024) in addition to Haiper (2024) which is winning the battle for being free. This seems to show that free is a trend with a view to engagement and then other types of subsequent monetization.

Without delving further into the universe of platforms and tools with AI engines that are launched daily, it can be established that it is possible to produce high-quality audiovisual content without using any type of voice, image, or acting talent

(Bazán-Gil, 2023). This implies that the only logistical element that would remain to be resolved would be distribution (Batlle, 2023). Due to the above, both advertising and pornography (both industries with complex ethical implications) are experimenting and investing in AI for the development of increasingly impactful and therefore more profitable audiovisual content (Madiega, 2019). The future of the audiovisual industry assisted by the Generative AI may involve prosumers developing entertainment products with high production values, giving rise to an emerging content industry leaving out the powerful audiovisual industry as happened with music production and record labels (Bern, 2023).

3.4 The Revolution of Artificial Intelligence in the Audiovisual Field and Human Security

The audiovisual dimensions of AI imply a revolution in the relationship between humans and machines. The relationship with machines has moved beyond mere experimentation to enter the realm of dialectical consciousness. The audiovisual work done with AI is experimental, evaluative, and propositional, achieving a transfer of shared knowledge. The transfer that AI produces is dialectical in that it allows for greater interaction and cooperation. Above all, AI achieves deep, reinforced, and shared learning.

The complexity of human consciousness, that is, a self-awareness that knows it is thinking, arises from the integration of visual and auditory stimuli combined with internal sensations that provoke self-thought. Internal sensations result from memory of contexts. AI is advancing toward having a semantic map of both local and global contexts to determine the nature of an event. From a video, AI correlates the meaning of an event with others within the same video, which allows for the generation of a meta-meaning of the video. An event within a video is structured with boundaries marked by the combination of image and sound (Wang et al., 2024a).

AI does not manually feed on individual frames to which a signifier (S1) is assigned; rather, it automatically extracts signifiers depending on the level of deep learning in the experiment, allowing for diverse interpretations of a particular frame and a chain of frames. Not only one command is assigned to a frame, but several signifiers can be accommodated. Simultaneously, alternative encoding and decoding universes come into play (Axyonov et al., 2024). However, the conscious revolution of AI lies in setting boundaries of meaning to events. The determination to set an interpretive limit to a frame or a series of frames comes from the automatic creation of the semantic map of the video. The synthesis capability of systems stems from their effectiveness in determining the assigned limits. AI is contextually aware due to its ability to set interpretation limits to an event, which is not exempt from error (Wang et al., 2024a).

Currently, AI applications are found in all areas of knowledge and praxis such as medicine, transportation, art, education, research, or finance, to name a few (Delgado et al., 2024). This is primarily due to three recent milestones: the mining, engineering, and processing of enormous amounts of data; the exponential advancement of technological tools; and primarily the development (paradoxically using AI) of increasingly sophisticated and precise algorithms (Searle, 2015, 2023; Bhargava and Sharma, 2022; Franganillo, 2023).

The transition of AI interaction with humans based on events in real contexts has occurred in all scenarios where experimentation and technical evaluation are possible. However, situations where AI not only provides efficiency in results for greater personal safety, but also enhances pleasurable experiences are of significant interest. This is evident in automated driving scenarios.

AI has enabled the development of automatic speech recognition technology. This plays a crucial role in hands-free interaction with car systems, improving driver comfort and promoting road safety. Audiovisual speech recognition is a revolution in accuracy, accessibility, and the growing development of natural communication between humans and machines.

The intelligent automatic speech recognition system (SR) is characterized by critical compression for refining resilience capabilities and by an increased sensitivity to context (Zhuang et al., 2020). By unlocking the potential of intelligent voice recognition systems, intuitive communication systems with cars capable of adopting personalized driving patterns are created. Improved experience includes in-car communication but goes beyond that, enhancing interaction in human–computer scenarios (Liang & Tang, 2022; Ouyang et al., 2023).

It has been challenging to unlock the potential of intelligent audio and video recognition systems because they are exposed to noisy contexts or situations where the captured image is obstructed. New systems incorporating AI have the flexibility to improve fact interpretation in scenarios with limited reliability elements. For example, in cases of excessive noise, the system focuses on video modality, but in low-light conditions or facial obstruction, it shifts toward audio (Ryumin et al., 2024). Experiments in complex environments using multitasking learning have surpassed conventional results to achieve high levels of recognition accuracy and flexibility through deep learning techniques in interaction with the driver (Kahn et al., 2020).

Automated intelligent vehicle driving through neural networks involves integrating experiments that work on lip occlusion. The challenge lies in the degraded capture of audiovisual recognition. There are various degrees of lip occlusion. AI allows for reconstructing occluded lip frames by including alternative images that match the perceived audio, thus obtaining high-fidelity images (Wang et al., 2024b). However, reinforced deep learning of neural networks allows for the generation of speaking faces, specifically constructing complete lips depending on audio quality, ensuring the information quality needed by the car to detect the driver's state in high-risk or crisis situations (Park et al., 2022).

With greater sensitivity to climate change issues, urban mobility has shifted toward the use of electric scooters and bicycles. However, health damages from vehicle pollution and user experiences with engine and tire noise are significant concerns. The need to create low-cost systems has led to integrating neural networks into existing navigation (GPS) systems to address health issues and provide a more satisfying experience (Al-Habaibeh et al., 2024).

The integration of sensors with neural networks allows for detecting harmful atmospheric particles, capturing sound waves, and revealing traffic density through images. Cameras, sensors, and GPS systems are integrated to build an association matrix through processing methods aimed at specifying sensor sensitivity, allowing for reality-based monitoring (Agudelo et al., 2021). Neural networks enable testing system accuracy.

Once the accuracy of the designed system is tested, neural networks allow transferring the model to other similar situations. Applying the model to more general conditions with common criteria is feasible. The result allows reliable monitoring of car effects on air quality, studying vehicle density in cities, and enhancing the experience of cyclists and electric scooter users through a low-cost system (Al-Habaibeh et al., 2024).

The increasingly close relationship between human and machine necessitates further work in cybersecurity. Deep reinforcement learning techniques have provided solutions to issues related to noticeable image quality loss when telecommunications service networks are saturated. Saturation due to a global increase in content demand not only affects image quality but also creates vulnerabilities to malicious attacks aimed at stealing sensitive user information (Net World, 2020). This is especially true during simultaneous interactions in video games (del Rio et al., 2024). Neural networks enable intelligent connectivity with high-quality multimedia audiovisual results at higher bitrates. The application of AI and automated learning techniques enhances high-performance in high-demand events and ensures higher cybersecurity indices for users (Zhou et al., 2020).

3.5 Ethical Considerations of Artificial Intelligence in the Audiovisual Field

The use of AI entails the establishment of ethical frameworks of action for all those involved. In this sense, the 193 Member States of UNESCO approved the First global agreement on the ethics of artificial intelligence in November 2021 (Naciones Unidas, 2021). The agreement established globally the first regulatory framework to promote human rights and contribute to the achievement of the Sustainable Development Goals with the use of AI, while prohibiting its use for social rating and mass surveillance (Naciones Unidas, 2021). Likewise, UNESCO (2022) made a recommendation on the values and principles that should be "respected by all actors during the life cycle of AI systems" (p. 18). The values are: (1) respect, protection, and promotion of human rights, fundamental freedoms, and human dignity; (2) prosperity of the environment and ecosystems; (3) ensuring diversity and inclusion; and (4) living in peaceful, just, and interconnected societies (UNESCO, 2022). We will talk about the principles later.

Now, specifically in the audiovisual industry, it should be noted that the use of increasingly powerful and sophisticate tools raises the possible design of an ethical framework that will have to be adjusted on the fly as problems arise (Vásquez Leal, 2020). An ethical scenario with regulation that does not compromise values, diversity and, above all, does not create new inequalities (Flores-Vivar & García-Peñalvo, 2023). In environments such as advertising or research, the observance of rights becomes obligatory (Pink, 2021), in the first by obligation and in the second by conviction. Advertising requires detailed image use and copyright contracts that aim to protect brands; an error or omission can mean million-dollar fines (Miramón & Murck, 2022). In the case of social science research with the development of visual and multimodal methods along with technology, the careful design of an ethical framework is imperative, to protect both the informants and the research itself (Carter, 2016; Pink, 2021).

One of the first reactions in the audiovisual industry was in copyright, leading human talents to claim their rights against an industry that could recreate them with AI after death (Vásquez Leal, 2020). Another problem for talents and artists has been the use of their image in sexual contexts or in the case of politicians and singers in the perfect reproduction of their voice to develop disinformation strategies (Rodríguez, 2023). Fortunately, there are cases of applications like Vidnoz (2024) that, although it performs digital facial superimposition or deepfake for free, prohibits the use of images and videos of violence or nudity.

In this regard, UNESCO has opened forums for the discussion of ethics in the audiovisual industry. SAG-AFTRA SAG-AFTRA includes two labor unions of the audiovisual industry which "represents approximately 160,000 actors, announcers, broadcast journalists, dancers, DJs, news writers, news editors, program hosts, puppeteers, recording artists, singers, stunt performers, voiceover artists and other media professionals" (SAG-AFTRA, 2024a). Duncan Crabtree-Ireland, SAG-AFTRA National Executive Director, as the keynote speaker in UNESCO's livestream panel, Artificial Intelligence in the Audiovisual Industry, talked about the risks and obligations of the companies in the use of AI in the audiovisual industry:

> the principles we fight for with respect to AI are simple. Each actor has just one face, just one voice. If the companies have free reign to train their AI algorithms on those faces and voices, then the actor's career could potentially be over. SAG-AFTRA is no opposed to the existence of AI technology and we won't be advocating for AI to be stopped or banned from use in the entertainment industry, but we do believe companies using AI technology must be required to secured the informed consent of any individuals whose voice, performance, likeness or intellectual property is being replicated or used to generate new material (UNESCO, 2023, 15m14s).

Duncan himself at the Stanford University Graduate School of Business "spoke to the necessity for legal safeguards as the technology continues to be developed. 'The reality is we need to have a balance that respects individuals and respects human creativity,'" (SAG-AFTRA, 2024b, par. 3–4). He also argues about the fourth industrial revolution as has been called this moment, and the problem of not being concern about ordinary people and workers (SAG-AFTRA, 2024b).

However, not all uses of AI are negative, as has been seen throughout this text. There are relevant contributions from the use and application of AI in the audiovisual industry for human safety and for the development of effective mobility that can positively impact the environment. Ethical considerations allow us to continue developing audiovisual solutions based on AI, based on the conceptualization that "ethics, as a philosophical discipline, has the mission of thinking about the present characterized by a continuous dominance of digital communication" (Del Prado, 2014).

We start from the fact that current communication happens in digital contexts, mediated by technology, but in which the social order is reproduced. In this sense, the application of artificial intelligence makes various things possible through the audiovisual field, solutions that in the end are part of the communication in which life in society is generated. We are faced with a fact comparable to Baudrillard's vision of the myth of consumption (2009) in which there is a discourse and an anti-discourse, a "critical mirage, the antifable that crowns the fable, the phrase and the antiphrase" (p. 250).

For all the above, it is important to integrate ethical and philosophical reflections around the 10 principles established by UNESCO (2022) for AI, as we will review below. Regarding the principle of proportionality and harmlessness, this involves evaluating the risks of AI to ensure it does not harm human beings, their rights, or their freedoms. It reflects precisely how what originally seeks to be beneficial could turn against them. This is why what Lipovetsky (1994) proposed three decades ago is still valid: it is up to the citizen to "face the contradictions of the system" (p. 19) or what Bauman (2004) said two decades ago: "The way that one lives becomes the biographical solution to systemic contradictions" (p. 91).

The principle of security and protection implies having sustainable data access frameworks, ensuring respect for privacy and promoting machine learning so that data is of higher quality (UNESCO, 2022). In this sense, it will be essential for people looking for solutions based on AI to share their findings and data so that others can use them. That is, taking advantage of AI for the common good, avoiding social indifference or lack of solidarity that arise structurally in society (Rorty, 1991). Consider the importance of the person in making decisions about what is communicated and how it is possible to create social and symbolic capital that makes collaboration possible (Arévalo-Martínez, 2019).

In terms of equity and non-discrimination, the benefits of AI must be promoted to be accessible to all. Bridging the digital divide and avoiding discriminatory or biased applications and results is a fundamental principle (UNESCO, 2022). That is, remember that global solidarity must prevail, responsibly seeking that everyone has the same opportunities for growth and development (Del Prado, 2018) in this case in the application of AI and its benefits.

Different international organizations have generated specific instances for Artificial Intelligence, among which we can say that the focus on three of the UNESCO principles (2022) stands out: (1) sustainability, which is the continuous evaluation of the effects of AI in all its dimensions, seeking to ensure that its application is in accordance with the United Nations Sustainable Development Goals; (2)

right to privacy, privacy, and data protection throughout the AI lifecycle; and (3) human oversight and decision in the sense that the AI system will never replace the ultimate responsibility of humans. These global institutions are the United Nations (Naciones Unidas, 2021) since the first global agreement on AI ethics, the World Economic Forum (2024) through the AI Governance Alliance, the OECD (2019) through its Global Initiative on Ethics of Artificial Intelligence, and the High-level expert group on artificial intelligence setup by the European Commission (2019), to mention a few.

Regarding the principle of transparency and explainability, it implies informing people in an adequate and timely manner when a decision is based on or made from AI, as well as sharing codes or data in some cases, making the results and the process to reach them understandable (UNESCO, 2022). This is of vital importance in the case of the use of AI in the audiovisual industry, first, in the generation of content, given the powerful influence that the media has on the way in which people perceive reality (Del Prado, 2016). Secondly, because of the possibility it generates for the democratization and sustainable development of other less favored regions or sectors, as well as independent producers that can compete with the monopolization of the industry. And thirdly, due to the need to have in all cases the informed consent of the people whose image, voice, or any of their creations were being recreated (UNESCO, 2023).

Regarding responsibility and accountability, it is important to protect and promote human rights and freedoms, the environment and ecosystems by becoming responsible and accountable in decisions or actions based on AI (UNESCO, 2022). Ensure auditability and traceability of AI systems. That is, to return to the existential condition of the humanist communicator who is committed to the truth and the best possible good for society (Del Prado, 2018).

In terms of awareness and education, media and information literacy of the public about AI should be promoted so that they can make informed decisions about the use of AI systems and are protected from undue influences (UNESCO, 2022). In this sense, it is worth remembering that the communicator is not the only one who has responsibility, but also the public who must know how to read, listen, and see (Del Prado, 2018). The training of active audiences with increasingly greater capabilities in the face of AI must be strengthened, to take advantage of it and, where appropriate, to protect themselves from being deceived.

With respect to the principle of adaptive and multi-stakeholder governance and collaboration, respect for international law and national sovereignty is sought, that is, the benefits of AI are shared for the sustainable development of all, taking care of respect for autonomy in the management of data for each person, including indigenous peoples (UNESCO, 2022). In this regard, as part of the audiences' rights, the national culture and the continuous contrast with other cultures must be considered to ensure the quality of the content and its plurality (Del Prado & Arévalo-Martínez, 2021).

3.6 Conclusion

We are facing an era of paradigm shift. As in any historical event, we must use new parameters to understand, take advantage of, and develop the capabilities that AI offers us. Above all, the integrity of the person and the search for the common good must prevail, there is no doubt about that. However, reflection is also necessary in the face of the risks that AI entails: substitution of activities that humans can perform, which would lead to unemployment; blindness to technological determinism with the consequent loss of the capacity for critical and purposeful thinking; as well as the loss of the social bond; to mention the most relevant ones.

This last element is fundamental in the ethical considerations of AI. Society is made up of people, people who communicate, people who, based on trust and interaction, build social, affective, and emotional ties. The intervention of AI in different processes of daily life can lead to a decrease in emotional ties, not only because people reduce their interaction and communication, but because it is impossible to establish this type of ties between the human being and the computer. Thus, strengthening human capabilities through AI, using it for solutions in the audiovisual industry, for health, safety, and environmental care, among others, will always be an added value if it does not go to the detriment of the development of society that is built by the bond between its members. We must move from simple interaction to the creation of links that generate community and make it possible for everyone to benefit (Arévalo-Martínez, 2021). Education in information and media literacy is essential for the production of person-centered communication, with ethics, social responsibility and search for the common good (Arévalo-Martínez et al., 2016), especially with the growing integration of AI in all areas of society.

References

Agudelo, O. E. A., Marín, C. E. M., & Crespo, R. G. (2021). Sound measurement and automatic vehicle classification and counting applied to road traffic noise characterization. *Soft Computing, 25*(2021), 12075–12087. https://doi.org/10.1007/s00500-021-05766-6

Aguilar, L. J. (2013). *Big data, Análisis de grandes volúmenes de datos en organizaciones*. Alfaomega.

Al-Habaibeh, A., Shakmak, B., Watkins, M., & Daniel Shin, H. (2024). A novel method of using sound waves and artificial intelligence for the detection of vehicle's proximity from cyclists and E-scooters. *MethodsX, 12*, 102534. https://doi.org/10.1016/j.mex.2023.102534

Arévalo-Martínez, R. I., Del Prado-Flores, R., & Ramírez-Beltrán, R. T. (2016). La formación institucional de investigadores en comunicación y la alfabetización mediática. El caso del Doctorado en Investigación de la Comunicación. *Revista Latina de Comunicación Social 71*, 800–817. https://doi.org/10.4185/RLCS-2016-1121.

Arévalo-Martínez, R. I. (2019). *Comunicación integral para las organizaciones: Liderazgo y creación de valor*. Comunicación Social Ediciones y Publicaciones.

Arévalo-Martínez, R. I. (2021). Comunicación digital para las organizaciones y responsabilidad social. *Sintaxis, 4*(2), 79–92. https://doi.org/10.36105/stx.2021edesp50aniv.01

Axyonov, A., Ryumin, D., Ivanko, D., Kashevnik, A., & Karpov, A. (2024). Audio-visual speech recognition in-the-Wild: Multi-angle vehicle cabin corpus and attention based method. In *IEEE International Conference on Acoustics, Speech and signal processing* (pp. 8195–8199). IEEE. https://doi.org/10.1109/ICASSP48485.2024.10448048

Barrere, R., Lautaro, M., Sokil, J., Trama, L. (2023). Desarrollo de la inteligencia artificial: Desafíos y oportunidades para la ciencia y la tecnología en Iberomérica. En *El Estado de la Ciencia. Principales indicadores de Ciencia y Tecnología Iberoamericanos/Interamericanos 2023* (pp. 27–39). Organización de Estados Iberoamericanos (OEI) y la Organización de las Naciones Unidas para la Educación, la Ciencia y la Cultura (UNESCO). https://www.ricyt.org/wp-content/uploads/2023/12/EL-ESTADO-DE-LA-CIENCIA-2023.pdf

Batlle, D. (2023, March 31). El boom de la Inteligencia Artificial: ¿Amenaza o salvación para la industria audiovisual? *ProQuest*. https://www.proquest.com/wire-feeds/el-boom-de-la-inteligencia-artificial-amenaza-o/docview/2793649392/se-2

Baudrillard, J. (2009). *La Sociedad del consumo. Sus mitos, sus estructuras*. Siglo XXI.

Bauman, Z. (2004). *La sociedad sitiada*. Fondo de Cultura Económica.

Bazán-Gil, V. (2023). Artificial intelligence applications in media archives. *Profesional de la Información, 32*(5), e320517. https://doi.org/10.3145/epi.2023.sep.17

Bhargava, C., & Sharma, P. (2022). *Artificial intelligence: Fundamentals and applications*. CRC Press.

Bordignon, F., Dughera, L., & Tolosa, G. (2023). IAG y el momento de las máquinas imperfectas. *Revista Hipertextos, 11*(19), 069. https://doi.org/10.24215/23143924e069

Boucher, P. (2020). *Intelligence: How does it work, why does it matter, and what can we do about it?* Scientific Foresight Unit. https://www.europarl.europa.eu/RegData/etudes/STUD/2020/641547/EPRS_STU(2020)641547_EN.pdf

Cádiz, R. F. (2020). Creating music with fuzzy logic. *Frontiers in Artificial Intelligence, 3*, 59. https://doi.org/10.3389/frai.2020.00059

Carter, D. (2016). Hustle and brand: The sociotechnical shaping of influence. *Social Media and Society*. doi:https://doi.org/10.1177/2056305116644144.

Ciucci, M., & Gouardères, F. (2020). *The White paper on Artificial Intelligence*. Policy Department for Economic, Scientific and Quality of Life Policies, European Parliament. https://www.europarl.europa.eu/RegData/etudes/BRIE/2020/648773/IPOL_BRI(2020)648773_EN.pdf

Del Prado, R. (2014). Ética y redes sociales. Introducción. En R. Del Prado (Coord.), *Ética y redes sociales* (pp. 7–17). Tirant Humanidades/Investigaciones y Estudios Superiores S.C.

Del Prado, R. (2016). *Ética y los derechos de las audiencias*. Limusa.

Del Prado, R. (2018). *Ética de la comunicación*. Gedisa-Universidad Anáhuac México.

Del Prado, R., & Arévalo-Martínez, R. I. (2021). Ética, política y derechos de las audiencias en México. Cómo olvidar a Foucault. *Logos. Revista de Filosofía, 49*(137), 63–83. https://repositorio.lasalle.mx/handle/lasalle/2233

del Rio, A., Serrano, J., Jimenez, D., Contreras, L. M., & Alvarez, F. (2024). Multisite gaming streaming optimization over virtualized 5G environment using Deep Reinforcement Learning techniques. *Computer Networks, 244*, 110334. https://doi.org/10.1016/j.comnet.2024.110334

Delgado, N., Campo Carrasco, L., Sainz de la Maza, M., & Etxabe-Urbieta, J. M. (2024). Aplicación de la Inteligencia Artificial (IA) en Educación: Los beneficios y limitaciones de la IA percibidos por el profesorado de educación primaria, educación secundaria y educación superior. *Revista Electrónica Interuniversitaria de Formación del Profesorado, 27*(1), 207–224. https://doi.org/10.6018/reifop.577211

ElevenLabs. (2024, July 27). *Generative Voice AI*. https://elevenlabs.io/

Europa Press. (2015, 12 de junio). *De Jurassic Park a Jurassic World: 22 años de evolución CGI*. Europa Press. https://www.europapress.es/portaltic/software/noticia-jurassic-park-jurassic-world-23-anos-evolucion-cgi-20150612124432.html

European Commission. (2019). *Independent high-level expert group on artificial intelligence*. European Commission. https://digital-strategy.ec.europa.eu/en/library/ethics-guidelines-trustworthy-ai

Flores-Vivar, J.-M., & García-Peñalvo, F.-J. (2023). Reflexiones sobre la ética, potencialidades y retos de la Inteligencia Artificial en el marco de la Educación de Calidad (ODS4). *Comunicar: Revista Científica de Comunicación y Educación, XXXI*(74), 37–47. https://www.revistacomunicar.com/pdf/74/c7403es.pdf

Foro Consultivo Científico y Tecnológico. (2018). *Inteligencia Artificial: Aplicaciones en la industria (INCYTU_18-012).* Foro Consultivo Científico y Tecnológico. https://www.foroconsultivo.org.mx/INCyTU/documentos/Completa/INCYTU_18-012.pdf

Franganillo, J. (2023). La inteligencia artificial generativa y su impacto en la creación de contenidos mediáticos. Methaodos. *Revista de Ciencias Sociales, 11*(2), m231102a10. https://doi.org/10.17502/mrcs.v11i2.710

Haiper. (2024, July 27). *Welcome to Haiper*. https://haiper.ai/onboarding

Harari, Y. N. (2024). (26 de junio de 2024). *AI, Future Tech, Society & Global Finance*. [Archivo de video]. Youtube. https://www.youtube.com/watch?v=_eYDNcSYUCA

HeyGen. (2024, July 27). *AI-powered video creation at scale*. https://www.heygen.com/

Hinojosa Becerra, M., Marín Gutiérrez, I., & Maldonado Espinosa, M. (2024). Inteligencia Artificial y la producción audiovisual. In Á. Torres-Toukoumidis & T. León-Alberca (Eds.), *ComunicAI. La revolución de la Inteligencia Artificial en la Comunicación* (pp. 117–136). Comunicación Social Ediciones y Publicaciones.

Kahn, J., Riviere, M., Zheng, W., Kharitonov, E., Xu, Q., Mazaré, P.-E., et al. (2020). Libri-light: A benchmark for ASR with limited or no supervision. In *Proceedings of the 2020 international conference on acoustics, speech and signal processing* (pp. 7669–7673). IEEE. https://doi.org/10.48550/arXiv.1912.07875

Liang, B., & Tang, Z. (2022). Multi-modal information analysis of automobile intelligent human-computer interaction. In *International conference on multi-modal information analytics* (pp. 658–666). Springer. https://doi.org/10.1007/978-3-031-05237-8_81

Lipovetsky, G. (1994). *El crepúsculo del deber. La ética indolora de los nuevos tiempos democráticos*. Anagrama.

Madiega, T. (2019). *EU guidelines on ethics in artificial intelligence: Context and implementation*. EPRS, European Parliament. https://www.europarl.europa.eu/RegData/etudes/BRIE/2019/640163/EPRS_BRI(2019)640163_EN.pdf

Miramón, F. G., & Murck, M. D. (2022). *#ChatarraInfluencer*. El Poder del Consumidor. https://elpoderdelconsumidor.org/2023/02/chatarrainfluencer/.

Naciones Unidas. (2021, 25 de noviembre). *Primer acuerdo mundial sobre la ética de la inteligencia artificial*. Noticias ONU. https://news.un.org/es/story/2021/11/1500522.

Nawaz, M., Javed, A., & Irtaza, A. (2023). Convolutional long short-term memory-based approach for deepfakes detection from videos. *Multimedia Tools and Applications*. doi:https://doi.org/10.1007/s11042-023-16196-x.

National Geographic España (2025, enero 16). *Breve historia visual de la inteligencia artificial*. https://www.nationalgeographic.com.es/ciencia/breve-historia-visual-inteligencia-artificial_14419.

Net World. (2020). *European technology platform, smart networks in the context of NGI, 2018*. https://www.networld2020.eu/wp-content/uploads/2018/11/networld2020-5gia-sria-version-2.0.pdf

Netflix. (2024, July 27). *Cómo funciona el sistema de recomendaciones de Netflix*. https://help.netflix.com/es/node/100639

Nevsky, A. (2023). Object-based access: Enhancing accessibility with data-driven media. *IMX 2023 - Proceedings of the 2023 ACM international conference on interactive media experiences* (pp. 402–406). doi:https://doi.org/10.1145/3573381.3596500.

OECD. (2019). *Artificial intelligence in society*. OECD Publishing. https://doi.org/10.1787/eedfee77-en

OpenAI. (2024, July 27). *Creating video from text*. https://openai.com/index/sora/

Ouyang, R., Ma, C., & Tan, H. (2023). The development of China automotive humancomputer interaction. In *International conference on human-computer interaction* (pp. 417–429). Springer. https://doi.org/10.1007/978-3-031-35939-2_31

Park, S. J., Kim, M., Hong, J., Choi, J., & Ro, Y. M. (2022). SyncTalkFace: Talking face generation with precise lipsyncing via audio-lip memory. In *Proceedings of the 36thAAAI conference on artificial intelligence* (pp. 234–778). https://doi.org/10.48550/arXiv.2211.00924x

Penrose, R. (2016). *The Emperor's new mind: Concerning computers, minds, and the laws of physics*. Oxford University Press.

Pink, S. (2021). *Doing visual ethnography*. Sage.

Prado-Hurtado, R. I. (2022). De lo personalizado a lo invasivo: retos actuales para la publicidad en medios electrónicos. En E. Leyva-Barcida, & G. A. Medina-Aguilar, *Comunicación organizacional para el siglo XXI* (pp. 151–171). Eólica Grupo Editorial.

Ramírez, V. (2018, marzo 7). House of Cards: el éxito que Netflix creó gracias a la inteligencia artificial. *Big Data Magazine*. https://bigdatamagazine.es/house-of-cards-el-exito-que-netflix-creo-gracias-a-la-inteligencia-artificial

Rey, G. T. (2023). *Pánico a los robots: El antecedente de miedo a la IA* (pp. 12–15). Historia y Vida.

Red de Indicadores de Ciencia y Tecnología Iberoamericana e Interamericana (RICYT). (2023). *El estado de la ciencia 2023*. https://www.ricyt.org/wp-content/uploads/2023/12/EL-ESTADO-DE-LA-CIENCIA-2023.pdf.

Rodríguez, D. F. (2023). *Huelga ante la liquidez de los derechos de propiedad intelectual e imagen en Hollywood*. Diario La Ley.

Rorty, R. (1991). *Contingencia, ironía y solidaridad*. Paidós.

Ryumin, D., Axyonov, A., Ryumina, E., Ivanko, D., Kashevnik, A., & Karpov, A. (2024). Audio–visual speech recognition based on regulated transformer and spatio–temporal fusion strategy for driver assistive systems. *Expert Systems with Applications, 252, Part A*. https://doi.org/10.1016/j.eswa.2024.124159

SAG-AFTRA. (2024a). *About*. https://www.sagaftra.org/about

SAG-AFTRA. (27 de junio de 2024b). *SAG-AFTRA NED Discusses Creators' Rights at Stanford University Panel on A.I.* https://www.sagaftra.org/sag-aftra-ned-discusses-creators%E2%80%99-rights-stanford-university-panel-ai

San Juan, P. B. (2023). Nuevas tecnologías y pornografía: la redimensión de la violencia sexual a través de la tecnología deepfake. En *V Simposio de Investigación Criminológica* (p. s.p.). Universidad de Málaga. https://hdl.handle.net/10630/27483

Searle, J. R. (2015). *Seeing things as they are: A theory of perception*. Oxford University Press.

Searle, J. R. (2023). *El misterio de la conciencia*. Paidós Studio.

Turing, A. M. (1905). *¿Puede Pensar Una Máquina?* Krk Ediciones.

UNESCO. (2022). *Recomendación sobre la ética de la inteligencia artificial*. https://unesdoc.unesco.org/ark:/48223/pf0000381137_spa

UNESCO. (19 de octubre de 2023). *Artificial intelligence in the audiovisual industry* [Video]. https://webcast.unesco.org/events/2023-10-AIAV/

Vásquez Leal, L. (2020). ¿Autoría algorítmica? Consideraciones sobre la autoría de las obras generadas por inteligencia artificial. *Revista Iberoamericana de la Propiedad Intelectual, 13*, 207–233. https://doi.org/10.26422/RIPI.2020.1300.vas

Vidnoz. (2024, julio 27). *Crear Vídeos con IA Gratis en 1 Minuto*. https://es.vidnoz.com/

Vilaça, L., Viana, P., Carvalho, P., & Andrade, T. (2020). Improving audiovisual content annotation through a semi-automated process based on deep learning. *Advances in Intelligent Systems and Computing, 942*, 66–75. https://doi.org/10.1007/978-3-030-17065-3_7

Volkswagen do Brasil. (2023, July 3). *VW 70 anos* | Gerações | VW Brasil. YouTube. https://www.youtube.com/watch?v=aMl54-kqphE

Wang, Y., Gao, W., Yang, S., Chen, Q., Ye, C., Wang, H., Zhang, Q., Ren, J., Ning, Z., Chen, X., Shao, Z., & Li, J. (2023). Humanoid intelligent display platform for audiovisual interaction and sound identification. *Nano-Micro Letters, 15*(1), 221. https://doi.org/10.1007/s40820-023-01199-y

Wang, H., Zha, Z.-J., Li, L., Chen, X., & Luo, J. (2024a). Context-aware proposal boundary network with structural consistency for audiovisual event localization. *IEEE Transactions on Neural Networks and Learning Systems, 35*(11), 15872–15882. https://doi.org/10.1109/TNNLS.2023.3290083

Wang, J., Pan, Z., Zhang, M., Tan, R. T., & Li, H. (2024b). Restoring speaking lips from occlusion for audio-visual speech recognition. *Proceedings of the AAAI conference on artificial intelligence, 38*(17), 19144–19152. https://doi.org/10.1609/aaai.v38i17.29882

World Economic Forum. (2024). *About AI governance alliance*. World Economic Forum. https://initiatives.weforum.org/ai-governance-alliance/about

Zhou, Y; Ling, L; Wang, L; , Hui, N; Cui, X; Wu, J; Peng, Y; Qi, Y; Xing, C. (2020). Service-aware 6G: An intelligent and open network based on the convergence of communication, computing and caching, Digital Communications and Networks (2020) 253–260, doi:https://doi.org/10.1016/j.dcan.2020.05.003.

Zhuang, F., Qi, Z., Duan, K., Xi, D., Zhu, Y., Zhu, H., et al. (2020). A comprehensive survey on transfer learning. *IEEE, 109*(1), 43–76. https://doi.org/10.1109/JPROC.2020.3004555

Rebeca-Illiana Arévalo-Martínez, Research Director at Universidad Anáhuac México. Member of the National System of Researchers (SNII) Level I at the Science, Humanities, Technology and Innovation Secretary in México since 2016. PhD in Applied Communication, Universidad Anáhuac México. Postdoctorate, Universidad de Málaga, España. Master in Corporate Communications with a Diploma in Branding and a Diploma in Active Methodologies, Universidad Anáhuac México. Graduate in Communication Sciences, Tecnológico de Monterrey.

Vice President of the Binational Association for Schools of Communication (BINACOM); Vice President for Latin America of the Modi Visual Association; Coordinator of GT2 Organizational Communication and Public Relations of the Latin American Association of Communication Researchers (ALAIC); former president of the Mexican Association of Researchers and Professionals in Organizational Communication (AMIPCO).

Winner of the Gold Quill Merit Award granted by the International Association of Business Communication (IABC) in 2001. Winner of the AMCO Award (Mexican Association of Communicators) in 1997 and 1998. Author and co-author of books, book chapters, articles, national presentations and international, scientific posters and thesis direction on research topics: digital organizational communication, leadership, organizational social responsibility, public relations, among others.

Rogelio del Prado Flores, Director of the Research Center for Applied Communication (CICA) and Academic Coordinator of the Research Communication PhD program, School of Communication at Universidad Anáhuac México certified by the of Science, Humanities, Technology and Innovation Secretary in Mexico. Professor and researcher at Universidad Autónoma de Baja California. Professor at the Master of Integral Communication and Social Transformation, Universidad Anáhuac México. Member of the National System of Researchers (SNII) Level 2 of the Science, Humanities, Technology and Innovation Secretary in México. PhD, Master and Graduate in Philosophy from UNAM, with honorable mentions in PhD and Master's degrees. He has a Postdoctorate in Communication Ethics, at the University of Seville, Spain.

He received the Alfonso Caso Silver Medal in 2004 for being the most distinguished graduate, a recognition granted by the UNAM Rectoral Council. He has the Pontifical Baccalaureate in Philosophy from the Pontifical University of Mexico.

Author of the books, Margins of Communication: Ethical Constitution of Intersubjectivity, edited by Tirant Lo Blanch; Communication Ethics, edited by Gedisa; Policies for Justice and communication, edited by Limusa. Coordinator of the books, Ethics and social networks; Ethics and rights of audiences; Co-editor of Humanizing technology, among others. Author and co-author of numerous articles, some of them published in Scopus, and in Web of Science.

Sintaxis Magazine's Editor. Magazine of the Research Center for Applied Communication, Universidad Anáhuac México.

Ricardo Ignacio Prado-Hurtado graduated with a degree in Advertising from the Centro de Estudios en Ciencias de la Comunicación (CECC), a Master's in Marketing from the Universidad Interamericana para el Desarrollo (UNID), and a PhD in Communication Research from the Universidad Anáhuac México. He also holds a PhD in Information and Communication Sciences from the Université Savoie Mont Blanc.

He serves as the Academic Coordinator of the Master in Integral Communication and Social Transformation and as a Research Professor at the Research Center for Applied Communication (CICA) at Universidad Anáhuac México.

He is associate researcher at the Laboratoire Langages, Littératures, Sociétés Estudes Transfotalières et Internationales (LLSETI) in France. Some of his research projects can be consulted at: https://www.cerealproject.org/ and https://www.metodos-visuales.mostro.mx/

He also has diplomas in Photography, Adobe trainer and Social Media. He was the General Director of Creative Services and a partner at Mostrotown Publicidad. With over 25 years working in the advertising field, he has managed some of the most renowned accounts in different product and service categories, such as Adidas Group, Grupo Bimbo, Colgate Palmolive, Disney, El Poder del Consumidor, Toyota, and World Wrestling Entertainment (WWE), among others.

He has been part of advertising, communication, and design agencies such as Draft, FCB, Sotomayor y Lara, Marketing Drive, Design Bureau, Kriptonita Advertising, Design Bureau, and Los Ángeles Carisma, among others.

He has specialized in social advertising and marketing, food studies, visual and multimodal methods, counter-marketing, and health communication, where he worked as a creative, art director, copywriter, and strategist for NGOs such as El Poder del Consumidor, Alianza por la Salud Alimentaria, and LatinNCAP.

He has collaborated as a teacher and speaker at universities such as Universidad Anáhuac México, Anáhuac Oaxaca, Anáhuac Mayab, Université Savoie Mont Blanc, Université de Lille, Centro de Estudios en Ciencias de la Comunicación, Instituto Politécnico Nacional, Universidad Iberoamericana, Universidad Intercontinental, and Universidad Interamericana para el Desarrollo.

Chapter 4
Implication of Artificial Intelligence in the Study Field of Neurocommunication and Media Literacy

Almudena Barrientos-Báez, David Caldevilla-Domínguez, and Felipe Chibás-Ortiz

4.1 Introduction

Just as ICTs have permeated and continue to permeate the population in all sectors of activity and at all levels of society, Artificial Intelligence is making its way along the same path. It is currently in the process of determining exactly in how many fields and in what way it will be a usable and practical technology. If what has happened with other digital technologies is indicative of anything, this path of transversality could easily reach the farthest reaches of professional and social activity (Abdullah et al., 2022; Agudelo González et al., 2022; Altamirano-Benítez et al., 2022), not only because of its link with communication, which is already the general binder of society (Pérez Valles & Reeves Huapaya, 2023).

In this case, AI is the new ICT, transversal even to communication itself, and therefore applicable to almost any field of human knowledge that seeks to expedite its creative, productive, and thought processes. The label "AI-assisted/created" has in fact become a brand name, giving rise to what is known as "AI washing." Referring to a process of washing or image adjustment applied to a product by labeling it as somehow associated with the phenomenon of Artificial Intelligence (Fernández Baón, 2023). In this sense, the need to clearly differentiate the real and realistic applications of the new technology, as opposed to the fictitious and fallacious ones, has become evident very soon; this is because the emergence of misleading applications for these new tools is almost inevitable. In the words of Arthur C. Clarke: "Any sufficiently advanced technology is indistinguishable from magic."

A. Barrientos-Báez (✉) · D. Caldevilla-Domínguez
Complutense University of Madrid, Madrid, Spain
e-mail: almbarri@ucm.es; davidcaldevilla@ccinf.ucm.es

F. Chibás-Ortiz
University of São Paulo, São Paulo, Brazil

A. Baraybar-Fernández et al. (eds.), *The AI Revolution*, Research Series on Responsible Enterprise Ecosystems, https://doi.org/10.1007/978-3-031-80411-3_4

And in the case of computer tools, the very limited understanding of how they work by a large part of the population makes them particularly vulnerable to this. It is for this reason that media and digital literacy is gaining importance with each new technological advance that takes place: because the application of these advances to the economic and social reality is increasingly faster, and there are no established mechanisms to educate the masses in their correct use and interpretation (Fernández et al., 2022).

The confluence of artificial intelligence (AI), neurocommunication, and media literacy represents a fascinating and increasingly relevant field of study in today's digital age. Artificial intelligence, with its ability to process and analyze large volumes of data at unprecedented speed and accuracy, has begun to play a crucial role in understanding and improving how humans process information and communicate (López López et al., 2023; Haidacher, 2020). This article explores the implication of AI in neurocommunication and media literacy, two areas that are intimately connected to how individuals access, process, and evaluate information in a variety of media.

Neurocommunication studies how the human brain interprets and responds to messages, while media literacy focuses on the ability to access, analyze, evaluate, and create information through various media. Both disciplines are essential to navigate and understand the vast information landscape that characterizes the twenty-first century (Cerdá Suárez & Cristófol Rodríguez, 2022). The integration of AI in these fields not only improves our understanding of the underlying cognitive processes, but also enhances media education, enabling a more personalized and effective approach to teaching and learning critical communication and analytical skills (Antón et al., 2022; Carral & Elías, 2024).

This paper aims to detail how artificial intelligence can be used to identify patterns in the way media is consumed and reacted to, and how it can support the creation of more effective communication strategies that are aligned with the neurological processes of the human brain. Through a comprehensive review of the literature, it seeks to provide a comprehensive view of the possibilities and challenges that AI poses in the transformation of neurocommunication and media literacy toward a more integrated and technology-supported model.

4.2 Objectives

The main objective of this scientific article is to develop a detailed analysis of how artificial intelligence (AI) is being integrated into the fields of neurocommunication and media literacy. Through a comprehensive review of the existing literature, it seeks to identify and analyze the theoretical foundations that interconnect AI with these emerging disciplines. This involves exploring how artificial intelligence technologies are being applied to enhance communication and information processing in neuroscientific and media literacy contexts. In addition, current applications of AI in these fields will be examined, highlighting case studies and practical examples where artificial intelligence has been implemented to optimize understanding and engagement in communication. The analysis will also extend to assess the effects and implications of these technologies on the way media information is received, processed, and interpreted.

This approach will provide a clear perspective on the potential of AI to transform neurocommunication and media literacy, thus contributing to the development of more effective and adaptive communication strategies in the digital age. In doing so, it is expected to contribute significantly to academic and practical knowledge, providing a solid foundation for future research and applications in these vital fields.

4.3 Methodology

A systematic and rigorous approach to scientific literature review was implemented to explore the implication of artificial intelligence (AI) in the fields of neurocommunication and media literacy. To conduct this review, relevant academic databases such as PubMed, IEEE Xplore, and Google Scholar were selected, mainly considering articles published between 2019 and 2024. Inclusion criteria focused on papers that explicitly addressed the integration of AI in neurocommunication studies and media literacy practices. Keywords such as "artificial intelligence," "neurocommunication," "media literacy," and "machine learning technologies" were used. The initial selection of papers underwent a screening process based on titles and abstracts, followed by a full-text analysis to ensure their relevance and contribution to the topic of study. This analysis identified predominant trends, technical and ethical challenges, and future opportunities at the intersection of these disciplines. The findings were synthesized and critically evaluated to provide a comprehensive perspective on the current state and future prospects for the use of AI in neurocommunication and media literacy, thus establishing a sound theoretical framework and a foundation for future research.

4.4 Results and Discussion

Artificial Intelligence (AI) is a branch of computer science that focuses on creating systems capable of performing tasks that would otherwise require human intelligence. These tasks can include reasoning, learning, perceiving, and understanding language (Rouhiainen, 2018). AI combines algorithms, large data sets, and often mimics the learning and problem-solving of the human brain, albeit with distinct capabilities and limitations (Forero-Corba & Bennasar, 2024).

Currently, the application of AI is extensive and has been integrated into numerous sectors. In the field of health, for example, AI contributes to medical diagnosis, helping to identify pathologies through medical images with an accuracy sometimes superior to that of humans (Basáez & Mora, 2022), being transversally affected by the phenomenon of digital hoaxes that AI has aggravated (Encinillas García & Martíon Sabarís, 2023; Soriano Guardia & Tramuns Fresnadillo, 2023). In the financial sector, advanced algorithms facilitate market analysis, manage investments, and detect fraud with an efficiency and speed unattainable for human analysts (Gimeno & Marqués, 2022). In commerce, AI personalizes the shopping experience by predicting consumer preferences based on their previous behavior and optimizes supply chains by accurately predicting demand (Adamssen, 2020).

AI is also transforming the automotive sector through the development of autonomous vehicles that promise to revolutionize the way we get around, increasing safety and reducing traffic congestion (Acevedo, 2023): a promise of dubious value if the underlying problem is not addressed: the complexity of the task for AIs, and the excessive number of personal automobiles (Huda et al., 2023). Moreover, in the field of education, adaptive AI tools are personalizing learning by adjusting content and pace according to the individual needs of each learner (García-Peñalvo et al., 2024).

It is thus evident how AI is redefining the boundaries of what is possible in various fields, promising not only to increase the efficiency of our activities but also to improve the quality of life globally. However, as this technology advances, important ethical and practical debates also arise that must be addressed to ensure its responsible integration into society (Cortina, 2022, p. 481):

> […] to distinguish between proposals that are scientifically supported by actual or possible experience, and those that do not have scientific backing. The first thing that an ethics of science, understood as an ethics of responsibility, demands is to make it clear that it is scientifically illegitimate to move from the first type of proposals to the second, treating them all as if they had scientific backing. It is a matter of practicing the critique of reason, which is the enlightened path towards reliable knowledge. This is because trust is indispensable for the functioning of societies, whether in the technosciences, in politics, in the economy or in the other activities of shared life.

In the field of education and professional training, AI has a role of particular interest for this study, transforming traditional methods and opening new possibilities for teaching and learning. Its application in education ranges from personalization of learning to automation of administrative tasks, offering opportunities to improve both educational efficiency and effectiveness (Flores et al., 2022). One of the most prominent applications of AI in education is the personalization of learning. Intelligent platforms use algorithms to analyze students' performance and learning styles, adapting learning material to suit their specific needs (Antón-Bravo & Serrano Tellería, 2021). This allows students to work at their own pace, delving deeper into topics they find challenging and advancing more quickly in areas where they show greater competence (Gómez, 2023, p. 223):

> AI allows adapting educational material according to the learner's needs and preferences (Peirats Chacón et al., 2018). Algorithms analyze collected data, such as academic performance, learning styles and individual interests, to provide specific and relevant content recommendations (Arboleya & Dopico, 2017). This means that students have access to educational resources tailored to their level of knowledge, learning pace and areas of interest, which facilitates their learning process and increases their motivation.

In addition, AI can help identify students at risk of school failure early, enabling more effective interventions. Through data analysis, intelligent systems can detect patterns that indicate learning difficulties or demotivation, alerting educators so that they can offer additional support when it is most needed (Guerrero-Roldán et al., 2020).

Another field that is highly affected is educational accessibility. AI is facilitating access to education for students with disabilities through tools such as enhanced screen readers, adaptive interfaces, and automatic translators that help break down language barriers and physical limitations (Sánchez & Catagna, 2021). Automation of administrative tasks is another area where AI is making a significant contribution. From automated test grading to schedule and resource management, AI allows educators and administrators to save valuable time, which can be redirected to more enriching teaching activities and direct interaction with students (Mejías et al., 2022).

AI is driving the development of immersive learning environments and complex simulations that were previously difficult to implement in the traditional classroom. These environments allow students to experience learning situations virtually, which is especially useful in disciplines such as medicine, engineering, and science, where hands-on experimentation can be costly or dangerous (Benavides et al., 2024).

The advent of AI in many aspects of daily and professional life has radically transformed the skills required in modern society. This has significantly increased the need for digital literacy, a fundamental skill for understanding and effectively using new technologies. As AI becomes integrated into fields such as medicine, commerce, education, and more, it becomes essential not only to know how to interact with these tools, but also to understand the basic principles behind them (Delgue, 2022). Digital literacy is not limited to the mere use of technological devices, but also involves a critical understanding of how these technologies work and affect society (Escoda et al., 2022). For example, in the workplace, AI-driven automation is redefining traditional roles and creating new jobs that require advanced skills in handling digital technologies. This demands from workers not only adaptability, but also a continuous ability to learn and manage new AI-based tools (Celaya & Campión, 2022). In addition, it makes other problems complex, such as greatly facilitating the generation of content for fake news (Vázquez Almendros & Paniagua Rojano, 2022).

In addition, digital literacy enables individuals to make informed and safe decisions online, where AI often personalizes what we see, from advertisements to news, based on algorithms that analyze our digital behavior (Zabala-Cia et al., 2022; Cueva Estrada et al., 2023). Understanding these mechanisms is crucial to critically navigate online content and protect personal privacy (Escoda et al., 2022, p. 239):

> It is important to emphasize that, for the proposal to be effective […] teachers must incorporate this work into their classroom dynamics in the way they consider most convenient in terms of timing (weekly, for example) and grouping (in groups or individually). The actions are designed to be carried out in any subject and with any syllabus, since they have been designed with a perspective of transversal application in Higher Education. Therefore, and by way of conclusions, it can be seen that the world has witnessed a global crisis in the flow of information and communications through the COVID-19, largely caused by social

networks, which has generated worldwide concern about the impact of fake news in societies. After several decades trying to alleviate this phenomenon in different contexts (European, national, etc.), the increase in the use of networks and the growing presence of the population in these spaces impose the need to face this problem from other perspectives, which involves the proper management of digital identity and consumption habits in networks and new formats of digital leisure and entertainment.

In the educational context, digital literacy helps students to take full advantage of AI-based educational tools, adapting to platforms that personalize learning and offer adaptive support according to the learner's needs. This not only improves learning effectiveness, but also prepares students for future work environments where AI will be a common tool (Benavides et al., 2024). In the civic sphere, finally, good digital literacy enables citizens to understand and question the ethical implications of AI, and the increasingly digitally mediated relationship with the state and administrations (Rodríguez, 2022).

Neurocommunication is an interdisciplinary field that studies how the human brain processes and understands communication. This term encompasses research on how people interpret language, images, sound, and other means of communication, and how these processes may be influenced by various neurological factors. It ranges from cognitive neuroscience to psychology and communication, seeking to understand the biological basis of communicative interaction and its impact on human behavior (Barrientos-Báez & Caldevilla-Domínguez, 2023). The history of the concept of neurocommunication dates back to the second half of the twentieth century, when advances in neuroscience began to allow a better understanding of the brain and its functions. As technologies such as functional magnetic resonance imaging (fMRI) and electroencephalography (EEG) became more accessible, researchers were able to take a closer look at how the brain reacts to different communicative stimuli. These technological advances provided powerful tools to explore the complex interactions between neurology and communication (Tinoco-Egas et al., 2020, p. 97):

> The measurement tools used could also be applied in neurocommunication and neuropolitical studies, among others. Electroencephalography (EEG) and electrodermal activity (EDA) solve business and marketing problems. Data obtained from consumer psychophysiology are often combined with measurements from self-assessments or questionnaires. Its applications are evident, as are the results it yields. Its growth goes hand in hand with technology, making it possible to understand essential patterns in consumers, delving into the depths of their mind in an unconscious way, with cognition taking a back seat. In spite of its praxis, it may entail increasing ethical problems, its constant use shows great challenges; therefore, its use and application must guarantee scientific rigor, and the demands of ethical considerations as a central guideline that defines favorable actions in the individual.

In recent decades, neurocommunication has grown as a field of study because of its potential to apply knowledge about the brain to improve communication strategies in areas such as marketing, education, speech therapy, and political communication. For example, neuromarketing, a subdiscipline of neurocommunication, uses knowledge about how the brain processes information to develop more effective marketing campaigns that can better capture the attention and interest of consumers

(Caldevilla-Domínguez et al., 2022). Neurocommunication also plays a crucial role in education and rehabilitation, helping to design teaching methods that better align with the way the brain learns and processes information.

From this context, customizing educational content—on media literacy in this case—using machine learning algorithms, AI can facilitate the implementation of curricula suited to individual neurological responses. For example, in the educational field, tools can be developed that adjust the didactic material in real time according to the student's brain response, optimizing the learning process by adapting to their style and pace (Sánchez et al., 2023):

> Regarding machine learning techniques, in relation to AI, grouping as a strategy would allow creating an early warning on those students who enter with a low level of prior knowledge necessary to face university mathematics, at the same time, it allows reviewing what should be the appropriate approach to present the information according to its type, order and emphasis. Regarding the recommendations of learning resources, based on the dimensions proposed by Felder and Silverman, it was found that there is no equality of criteria among the authors, so a new table summarizing these approaches was proposed. Mainly, for the global/sequential dimension, there is no clarity regarding the most appropriate type of resource, but this information can be used to select the order in which the resources are presented.

In this regard, the potential of the new technology reaches to facilitate the analysis and classification of the way in which consumers respond emotionally to different communicative stimuli. Using neurocommunication techniques, such as measuring brain activity and physiological responses, AI can help predict and improve the emotional impact and attention of advertising campaigns (Wijntjes, 2012). Finally, AI can also improve the accessibility of communication for people with hearing or visual impairments. For example, it can develop and improve speech-to-text recognition systems or automatic sign language translation, facilitating inclusive communication (Baldiris et al., 2015) fundamentally affecting power dynamics in the digital sphere, as understood by Pérez Altable & Serrano-Tellería (2021).

Although it may sound like science fiction, brain–computer interface machines exist and have the potential to be enhanced by AI. This can be seen from the possibility of its use for teaching assessment in students (Ferreira et al., 2021) and for the improvement of the living conditions of the disabled, which has been under development for some time (Guevara Mosquera, 2012).

4.5 Conclusion

The relationship between artificial intelligence (AI) and neurocommunication represents one of the challenges and keys to the future, encompassing the study of how machines can simulate human neurological processes to improve communication and understanding between humans and computational systems. AI is inspired by the structure and function of the human brain to develop algorithms and models that can perform machine learning, natural language processing, and pattern recognition tasks, among others. Neurocommunication, on the other hand, studies how neural processes affect communication and behavior, exploring ways to apply this knowledge to improve human or machine interaction.

AI can benefit from neurocommunication insights by using models based on brain functioning to create more intuitive and natural interfaces, thus facilitating human–machine interaction. For example, AI systems can apply neurocommunication principles to recognize and respond to human emotional signals, improving the ability of machines to understand and anticipate user needs.

Similarly, neurocommunication can leverage advances in AI to analyze large volumes of data on brain activity and communicative behavior, opening up new insights into understanding how the brain processes and generates communication. This includes the development of brain–computer interface technologies that enable direct communication between neural activity and electronic devices, which has significant implications for medical rehabilitation, enhanced learning, and social interaction. The synergy between AI and neurocommunication promises not only to enrich our understanding of the human mind and its communication processes, but also to advance the creation of technologies that are more adaptive and responsive to the complexities of human behavior and emotions.

Artificial intelligence (AI) can really change the game in the world of media literacy, making it more personalized, interactive, and accessible to all. Imagine that every time you learn about media, the content automatically adapts to the user's interests or what the user most needs to improve. That's something AI can do, adjusting learning materials to perfectly match the learner—helping him or her, for example, in the process of discerning the modern flood of false information provided by ICT.

In this regard, the role of AI would be to help us identify what is real and what is not, teaching us to be more critical of what we read or see online. Creating content also becomes much easier with AI. Whether it's the process of making a video, writing an article or designing an infographic, there are AI-powered tools that can help your work stand out, making it easier and more fun. AI also makes learning about media easier and more fun, thanks to intelligent user interfaces that can guide the user through your learning with chatbots or recommend new topics based on their interests and progress. It's a 24/7 assistant, available to discuss—or rather, analyze—ideas, refine concepts, and create templates for designing every page and every interaction, particularly in written content creation.

And let's not forget how AI can provide instant feedback. This is like having a personal tutor explaining exactly what to improve and how, making the learning process much more effective. Finally, AI breaks down barriers, allowing you to access media literacy resources from all over the world, no matter what language they are written in, opening up a world of knowledge and perspectives.

As noted in the introductory section, technology is not going to stop evolving: if the metaverse doesn't crash the Zuckerberg legend, one day it will be the next big thing to come flooding in and changing our lives. On that day, perhaps knowing how to insert the right prompts into an AI interface will help us manage and understand the new technology more deeply and in a more evenly distributed way on a societal level. But to do so, it will require awareness of the importance of maintaining technological competence and continued media skepticism throughout an individual's life trajectory. Because no matter how personalized the learning experience is or how simple the user interface is a priori, the truth remains that it is not possible to teach those who do not wish to learn.

Acknowledgments This text is part of a CONCILIUM project (931.791) of the Complutense University of Madrid, "Validation of models of communication, neurocommunication, business, social networks and gender."

References

Abdullah, N. H., Hassan, I., Azura Tuan Zaki, T. S., Ahmad, M. F., Hassan, N. A., Mohd Zahari, A. S., Ismail, M. M., & Azmi, N. J. (2022). Examining the relationship between factors influencing political information seeking-behaviour through social media among youths in Malaysia. *Revista de Comunicación de la SEECI, 55*, 1–15. https://doi.org/10.15198/seeci.2022.55.e746

Acevedo, M. E. C. (2023). Desarrollo de modelos vehículo-conductor para vehículos articulados utilizando inteligencia artificial. *Laboratorio Nacional CONAHCYT en Electromovilidad Inteligente, 2*(1) https://cv.cicataqro.ipn.mx/dsm/index.php/biocq/article/view/4/2

Adamssen, J. (2020). *Inteligencia artificial: Aprender sobre chatbots, robótica y otras aplicaciones comerciales*. Efalon Acies.

Agudelo González, L. E., Marta-Lazo, C., & Aguaded, I. (2022). Competencias digitales en el Currículo de Periodismo: Análisis de caso de una universidad Centroamericana. *Vivat Academia, 155*, 297–316. https://doi.org/10.15178/va.2022.155.e1393

Altamirano-Benítez, V., Ruiz-Aguirre, P., & Baquerizo-Neira, G. (2022). Política 2.0 en Ecuador. Análisis del discurso y la comunicación política en Facebook. *Revista Latina de Comunicación Social, 80*, 201–223. https://doi.org/10.4185/RLCS-2022-1539

Antón, L. A., Fernández, Á. F., & Rodríguez, I. S. (2022). Las tendencias Edtech para la alfabetización mediática en el aula. Herramientas de fact-checking. *Aula de Encuentro, 24*(2), 50–69. https://doi.org/10.17561/ae.v24n2.7102

Antón-Bravo, A., & Serrano Tellería, A. (2021). Innovación en la docencia del periodismo a través de la ciencia de datos. *European Public & Social Innovation Review, 6*(1), 70–84. https://pub.sinnergiak.org/esir/article/view/150

Arboleya, E., & Dopico, E. (2017). Superando las barreras físicas del aula: recursos naturales y TIC. *Revista Iberoamericana de Educación, 75*(1). https://doi.org/10.35362/rie7511356

Baldiris, S., Fabregat, R., Cuesta, J., Muñoz, T., & Cardona, S. (2015). CO-CREARIA: Modelo de co-creación de REA inclusivos y accesibles. *Ingeniería e Innovación, 3*(2), 39–48. https://shorturl.at/hwDK2

Barrientos-Báez, A., & Caldevilla-Domínguez, D. (2023). Neurocomunicación en videojuegos: llegando a un público sobreestimulado. *Techno Review. International Technology, Science and Society Review/Revista Internacional de Tecnología, Ciencia y Sociedad, 13*(4), 1–13. https://doi.org/10.37467/revtechno.v13.4809

Basáez, E., & Mora, J. (2022). Salud e inteligencia artificial: ¿cómo hemos evolucionado? *Revista Médica Clínica Las Condes, 33*(6), 556–561. https://shorturl.at/aenCK

Benavides, J. P. C., Chávez, C. A. C., & Arcos, Á. X. T. (2024). El uso de la inteligencia artificial en la creación de entornos de aprendizaje inmersivos en la educación superior. *Revisión sistemática. RECIAMUC, 8*(1), 348–356. https://shorturl.at/hruBX

Caldevilla-Domínguez, D., Barrientos-Báez, A., García-Manso, A., & Matarín-Rodríguez-Peral, E. (2022). Neurocomunicación y Manosferas: estudio de caso Forocoches. *Historia y Comunicación Social, 27*(2). https://doi.org/10.5209/hics.84402

Carral, U., & Elías, C. (2024). Aplicación de herramientas de IA como metodología para el análisis de la toxicidad en la conversación en redes sociales: Estudio de caso de la política española en Twitter. *Revista Latina de Comunicación Social, 82*, 1–18. https://doi.org/10.4185/rlcs-2024-2205

Celaya, L. A. A., & Campión, R. S. (2022). *El reto de la alfabetización digital: de la sustitución a la transformación* (Vol. 10). Editorial UOC.

Cerdá Suárez, L. M., & Cristófol Rodríguez, C. (2022). Un estudio exploratorio sobre el impacto del neuromarketing en entornos virtuales de aprendizaje. *Vivat Academia, Revista de Comunicación, 155*, 1–16. https://doi.org/10.15178/va.2022.155.e1391

Cortina, A. (2022). Los desafíos éticos del transhumanismo. *Pensamiento. Revista de Investigación e Información Filosófica, 78*(298), 471–483. https://shorturl.at/dQ368

Cueva Estrada, J. M., Sumba Nacipucha, N., Meleán Romero, R., Artigas Morales, W., Cueva Ortiz, N., & Plaza Quimis, M. (2023). Gestión del contenido en redes sociales, por revistas científicas indexadas en SciELO España. *Revista de Comunicación de la SEECI, 56*, 194–213. https://doi.org/10.15198/seeci.2023.56.e834

Delgue, J. R. (2022). Alfabetización digital para el Metaverso. *Noticias Cielo, 12*(10), 1–2. https://shorturl.at/qAPT8

Encinillas García, M., & Martín Sabarís, R. (2023). Desinformación y Salud en la era PRECOVID: Una revisión sistemática. *Revista de Comunicación y Salud, 13*, 1–15. https://doi.org/10.35669/rcys.2023.13.e312

Escoda, A. P., Fernández, E. A. O., & Esteban, L. M. P. (2022). Alfabetización digital para combatir las fake news: Estrategias y carencias entre los/as universitarios/as. *Prisma Social: Revista de Investigación Social, 38*, 221–243. https://shorturl.at/ltADQ

Fernández Baón, R. (17/10/2023). ¿Qué es el AI-washing?. *Marketing4all.es*. https://shorturl.at/atBT4

Fernández, Á. F., Antón, L. A., & Rodríguez, I. S. (2022). El papel de las narraciones digitales interactivas en los procesos de alfabetización mediática y comunicacional. *Etic@ net. Revista científica electrónica de Educación y Comunicación en la Sociedad del Conocimiento, 22*(1), 70–89. https://doi.org/10.30827/eticanet.v22i1.24065

Ferreira, A. C., Santiago, M. A., & Ortega, M. D. L. Á. L. (2021). Empleo de dispositivos BCI en alumnos para la evaluación docente. *RIED-Revista Iberoamericana de Educación a Distancia, 24*(1), 315–328. https://shorturl.at/jnFW8

Flores, F. A. I., Sánchez, D. L. C., Urbina, R. O. E., Coral, M. Á. V., Medrano, S. E. V., & Gonzales, D. G. E. (2022). Inteligencia artificial en educación: una revisión de la literatura en revistas científicas internacionales. *Apuntes Universitarios, 12*(1), 353–372. https://shorturl.at/acOS6

Forero-Corba, W., & Bennasar, F. N. (2024). Técnicas y aplicaciones del Machine Learning e Inteligencia Artificial en educación: una revisión sistemática. *RIED-Revista Iberoamericana de Educación a Distancia, 27*(1) https://shorturl.at/tFH17

García-Peñalvo, F. J., Llorens-Largo, F., & Vidal, J. (2024). La nueva realidad de la educación ante los avances de la inteligencia artificial generativa. *RIED-Revista Iberoamericana de Educación a Distancia, 27*(1), 9–39. https://shorturl.at/cdivG

Gimeno, R., & Marqués, J. M. (2022). Tradición e inteligencia artificial: oportunidades y retos del machine learning para los servicios financieros. *ICE, Revista de Economía, 926*, 109–118. https://shorturl.at/BIQT2

Gómez, W. O. A. (2023). La inteligencia artificial y su incidencia en la educación: Transformando el aprendizaje para el siglo XXI. *Revista internacional de pedagogía e innovación educativa, 3*(2), 217–229. https://shorturl.at/puvxV

Guerrero-Roldán, A. E., Rodríguez, M. E., Bañeres, D., Pérez, C., Panadero, J., & Karadeniz, A. (2020). Hacia un sistema de detección temprana de estudiantes en riesgo en entornos de enseñanza-aprendizaje en línea. En J. M. Badía Contelles, F. Grimaldo Moreno (eds.), *Actas de las XXVI Jornadas sobre la Enseñanza Universitaria de la Informática*, València, 8–9 de julio de 2020. Asociación de Enseñantes Universitarios de la Informática, 37–44. https://shorturl.at/iwV49

Guevara Mosquera, S. D. (2012). *Adquisición de señales electroencefalográficas para el movimiento de un prototipo de silla de ruedas en un sistema BCI* [Bachelor's thesis] Universidad Politécnica Salesiana de Ecuador. https://shorturl.at/uPR39

Haidacher, S. (2020). *Verkauf durch Emotionen: In der Phase der Kundenansprache durch den Außendienst im B2B am Beispiel von L'Oréal und dem Salon Emotion-Konzept* [Disertación doctoral]. Fachhochschule der Wirtschaft. https://shorturl.at/ajs24.

Huda, F. Y., Currie, G., & Kamruzzaman, M. (2023). Understanding the value of autonomous vehicles–an empirical meta-synthesis. *Transport Reviews, 43*(6), 1058–1082. https://shorturl.at/zHJO9

López López, P. C., Mila Maldonado, A., & Ribeiro, V. (2023). La desinformación en las democracias de América Latina y de la península ibérica: De las redes sociales a la inteligencia artificial (2015-2022). *URU, Revista de Información y Cultura, 8*, 69–89. https://revistas.uasb.edu.ec/index.php/uru

Mejías, M., Coronado, Y. C. G., & Peralta, A. L. J. (2022). Administración y Educación sobre la Inteligencia Artificial en el campo de la enfermería. *Revista Conrado, 18*(S4), 284–290. https://shorturl.at/exFR7

Peirats Chacón, J., Marín Suelves, D., Granados Sáiz, J., & Morote Blanco, D. (2018). Competencia digital en los planes de estudio de universidades públicas españolas. *REDU. Revista de Docencia Universitaria, 16*(1), 175–191. https://doi.org/10.4995/redu.2018.8935

Pérez Altable, L., & Serrano-Tellería, A. (2021). Communications patterns and power dynamics in the digital public sphere: A case study of the conversation about Minimum Living Income on Twitter. *European Public and Social Innovation Review, 6*(1), 1–15. https://pub.sinnergiak.org/esir/article/view/148

Pérez Valles, C., & Reeves Huapaya, E. (2023). Educación inclusiva digital: Una revisión bibliográfica actualizada. Las brechas digitales en la educación inclusiva. *Actualidades Investigativas en Educación, 23*(3), 3–28. https://doi.org/10.15517/aie.v23i3.54680

Rodríguez, A. L. T. (2022). Ética para la inteligencia artificial sostenible. *Arbor, 198*(806), a683–a683. https://shorturl.at/nxCRZ

Rouhiainen, L. (2018). *Inteligencia artificial*. Alienta Editorial.

Sánchez, L. A. C., & Catagña, S. M. C. (2021). La educación virtual implementada por la pandemia de la COVID-19 y el derecho a la educación superior. *Revista Jurídica Crítica y Derecho, 2*(3), 44–56. https://shorturl.at/jtx05

Sánchez, J. S. P., Pardo, I. D. T., & de Meriño, C. Y. M. (2023). Personalización de recursos para la enseñanza de matemáticas universitarias usando inteligencia artificial. *Revista Interamericana de Investigación Educación y Pedagogía RIIEP, 16*(1), 319–340. https://shorturl.at/gwzQ5

Soriano Guardia, J., & Tramuns Fresnadillo, A. (2023). Vacunas contra la COVID-19 en España: disposición de la población a vacunarse y sus principales preocupaciones e ideas equivocadas. *Revista de Comunicación y Salud, 14*, 10.35669/rcys.2024.14.e340.

Tinoco-Egas, R., Juanatey-Boga, Ó., & Martínez-Fernández, V. A. (2020). Neuromarketing: Consideraciones teóricas y herramientas de medición. *Revista Venezolana de Gerencia, 25*(90), 613–631. https://shorturl.at/fCMU2

Vázquez Almendros, P., & Paniagua Rojano, F. J. (2022). La labor de verificación de noticias desde el departamento de comunicación. Estudio de casos en el sector agroalimentario. *Revista de Ciencias de la Comunicación e Información, 27*, 33–55. https://doi.org/10.35742/rcci.2022.27.e238

Wijntjes, M.-J. (2012). *African studies companion online*. De Gruyter. https://shorturl.at/CPWX9

Zabala-Cia, O., Lorenzo-Sola, F., & González-Pacanowski, T. (2022). Interactividad en redes sociales para crear relaciones de confianza: ayuntamientos de Navarra en tránsito. *Revista de Ciencias de la Comunicación e Información, 27*, 23–43. https://doi.org/10.35742/rcci.2022.27.e246

Almudena Barrientos-Báez, Advisor to the Vice-rectorate of Research and Transfer for the support to the development of action lines of the Complutense University of Madrid (UCM). Teacher at the Faculty of Information Sciences of the Department of Theories and Analysis of Communication at the Complutense University of Madrid. Doctor with international mention Cum Laude in Education. Former Director of the Master's Degree in Teacher Training at the European University of Madrid. Master in Protocol Management, Production, Organization and Design of Events—area of COMMUNICATION—(Univ. Camilo José Cela) and Master in Tourism Accommodation Management (Univ. Girona). Degree in Tourism (Univ. of La Laguna) and Diploma in Teaching (Univ. Valencia). Her research work is directly and transversally linked to Neuromarketing, Neurocommunication, Gender, Social Networks, Communication, PR and ICT. She is part of the Public audiovisual media project in the platform ecosystem: management and evaluation models of the reference public value for Spain, (PID2021-122386OB-I00), funded by the MCIN, AEI and FEDER, EU. Ministry of Science and Innovation and member of the Research Team: Communication and Education Office. Department of Journalism and Communication Sciences of the UAB.

David Caldevilla-Domínguez, He is a Professor, Graduate and Doctor in Information Sciences, (Audiovisual Communication from the Univ. Complutense). Diploma in Teaching (U. of Zaragoza). Two sexennials (2006–2018). Teacher at: Univ. Complutense, European Univ. of Madrid, IED, ESERP and IPAM (Oporto-Portugal-). With more than 20 subjects. Speaker and lecturer in various courses and professor in several own titles (Telemadrid, Walter & Thompson, McCann...). Secretary General of the Spanish Society of Ibero-American Communication Studies (SEECI), of the "International Fórum of Communication and Public Relations" (Fórum XXI) and of "History of information systems" (HISIN). Principal Investigator (I.P.) of the Complutense Research Group 'Concilium' with number 931,791. Researcher in more than 15 official research projects. Author of more than 100 scientific articles in peer-reviewed journals, more than 55 book chapters and 6 complete books: Asturias and La Rioja, a common history, Spielberg's seal, Culture and Public Relations, Public Relations Manual, The Relations Public and its foundation and The internal face of business communication. Director of 9 doctoral theses. Member of scientific committees in numerous international scientific conferences and journals.

Felipe Chibás-Ortiz, He is the Latin American and Caribbean Representative of the Global Alliance for Partnerships on Media and Information Literacy (GAPMIL) of UNESCO. He is an Associate teacher (2015) and holds a PhD in Communication Sciences from Faculty of Coomunication and Arts of the University of São Paulo – USP(2005), a master's degree in Culture and Communication from the Latin American Integration Program (PROLAM) from USP (2000) and a degree in Psychology from the University of La Habana Also specialization in Direct Marketing from the Alcalá de Henares University in Spain (2010). He is a teacher at the Center for Evaluation and Measurement Studies in Communication and Marketing (CEACOM) at the University of São Paulo. In the postgraduate courses in Communication and Marketing Management, Political Marketing and Integrated Communication Management in digital environments, He teaches the subjects of Innovation Management and Organizational Creativity, Public Speaking and Personal Marketing and Design Thinking, respectively. He also taught at ECA- USP the disciplines of Marketing, Organizational Culture and Corporate Identity for undergraduate courses in Advertising and Public Relations. Coordinates the study group Thot-CRIARCOM (Creativity, Innovation, Communication and Marketing). See www.criarcom.com. In graduate school at Presbyterian University. Mackenzie teaches Business Management, Organizational Change and Digital Marketing, among others.

Chapter 5
Creativity in the AI Revolution

Jesús Plaza

5.1 Introduction

In a world where the boundaries between reality and fiction blur more each day, we find ourselves on the brink of an unprecedented revolution. Artificial intelligence (AI) is not only transforming the audiovisual industry; it is changing the very essence of our creativity, our perception, and ultimately, our humanity. This is not just another revolution; it is the crossroads between the tangible and the digital, between art and algorithm. It is the story of how AI is rewriting our world, one line of code at a time.

Imagine a dawn in a world where digital cameras are relics of a distant past, replaced by the omnipresence of AI. The streets of cities, once filled with photographers and filmmakers, are now populated by artists who converse with their artificial intelligences, creating masterpieces in the blink of an eye. We are living in an era comparable to the invention of the film camera or the advent of the digital camera, but with a magnitude and speed that leave those revolutions in the shadows. This revolution is redefining our life goals, our professions, and even our dreams. And it's happening so fast we're not even aware of it. Previous industrial revolutions took shape and were established over longer periods and, although they were also disruptive to a society that had to adapt, this revolution we are experiencing is like all the previous ones combined and multiplied by ten. One key difference for me is that everything is already in place for this revolution to be effective in a very short time. All the necessary elements already exist: the internet, the technology we need, smartphones, connectivity … we just need to finish developing the AI. But don't fall asleep, because it will arrive before you realize it.

J. Plaza (✉)
Sony Pictures, Madrid, Spain

A. Baraybar-Fernández et al. (eds.), *The AI Revolution*, Research Series on Responsible Enterprise Ecosystems, https://doi.org/10.1007/978-3-031-80411-3_5

5.2 Objectives

The purpose of this analysis is to shed light on this inevitable revolution. We aim to unravel how AI is affecting creative processes in the audiovisual industry, identify the main beneficiaries and those affected, and provide an optimistic and practical perspective on how to ride this technological wave instead of being swept away by it. In the end, the question is not if we will adapt, but how we will do it. Because those who don't adapt will be left behind. And this raises another very interesting reflection: in a world where everything is possible and instantaneous, everyone will be able to create impactful images or videos, but will everyone do it? And then what will have value? I believe that creators will benefit the most from these tools and that more people will be able to create, but we will still value pieces that have a concept, a story, soul, that impact you. So, not everything will be good; within the sea of creations, we will have to see which ones are good, and there the human factor will remain important.

5.3 The Impact of AI on the Audiovisual Industry

AI has not come to steal the spotlight; it has come to be the star. At a dizzying speed, thanks to the already existing technological infrastructure, AI is generating an explosion of unprecedented creativity. Imagine a world where tools like ChatGPT, Runway, Midjourney, Freepik, Magnific, and others not only assist creators but collaborate with them as equals. In this new landscape, individuals and small teams have the ability to create high-quality audiovisual content more quickly and efficiently. "Artificial intelligence is fundamentally transforming the audiovisual industry, accelerating content production while enabling new creative possibilities that were previously unimaginable." (Smith, 2021, p. 56).

The adoption of AI is happening faster than we can comprehend. Every day, thousands of people discover new ways to integrate AI into their creative processes. The result? A democratization of creativity where anyone, with the right tool, can produce something worthy of a film festival. But what does this mean for the industry? And are all results equally valid and valuable?

5.3.1 Beneficiaries and Affected

In this new ecosystem, the main beneficiaries will be those with an innate passion for storytelling: artists, creators, and storytellers. AI amplifies their creative capabilities, allowing them to materialize visions that were previously difficult or impossible to achieve alone. Picture an independent filmmaker who, armed with AI, can produce a work that rivals those of major studios, all from the comfort of their home. It sounds crazy or like a distant scenario, but we've already seen similar cases of very young people using tools like Blender or After Effects, capable of creating sequences worthy of Netflix. "The integration of AI tools such as generative algorithms not only boosts the speed of production but also provides creators with novel ways to visualize and execute their artistic vision." (Johnson & Lewis, 2020, p. 23).

However, this change will also bring the loss of some jobs and the transformation of others. Technicians and professionals who were once indispensable might find their skills replaced by faster and more precise algorithms. But not everything is pessimistic. This change will generate a new set of challenges and opportunities in the sector, where those who adapt will thrive. That's why one of the keywords of this new revolution is adaptability. We must be able to evolve with the revolution and become valuable in a constantly changing society.

5.3.2 *Adaptability: Changes in the Creative Paradigm*

We are entering an era where fast and low-cost creations, compared to "churros," will coexist with high-quality, meticulously controlled productions, the "bio muffins." AI will allow creators to produce content with unprecedented efficiency, but at a cost: the loss of a certain degree of control and quality. "AI-driven creativity blurs the line between human and machine capabilities, creating a space where collaborative workflows lead to content that is more engaging and accessible." (Roberts et al., 2019)

For those who want a quick production, it will be necessary to sacrifice the meticulousness and detail that only a professional team dedicating time and care to the work can offer. However, more elaborate productions will require time, knowledge, and economic effort, thus redefining industry standards and public perception of what constitutes quality content. Imagine a film where every frame is a testament to human ingenuity enhanced by AI precision. This is the new cinema, where human creativity and AI efficiency intertwine to create something truly magical. Now apply it to advertising, music videos, short films, and so on.

5.3.3 *Ethical Challenges and Responsibilities*

With the increase in creative capacity also comes a greater ethical responsibility. The ease of creating hyper-realistic content will increase the risks of deep fakes and online fraud, making it more difficult to discern reality from fiction. Can we trust what we see? Young people, in particular, will feel increasing pressure from the unrealistic standards promoted on social media. Electoral fraud, fake news, scams … we are entering a truly delicate era.

The responsibility lies with us, the creators, to develop a critical and ethical sense in the use of these technologies. We must be guardians of truth and authenticity in a world where the line between the real and the fabricated becomes increasingly blurred. Human creativity must be the compass that guides us through this new digital landscape, and human values its pillars.

5.3.4 Generative AI: Wings for the Imagination

Generative AI is giving wings to the imagination of millions of creative people who have always wanted to tell their stories. These tools expand the set of tools available to creators, making them more accessible than ever. For example, Midjourney and Runway allow high-quality images or videos to be generated from simple textual descriptions, while ChatGPT can generate scripts and dialogues with surprising coherence and fluidity. These tools increasingly fulfill more functions, becoming more complete and erasing technical difficulties by approaching pure language to communicate with creators.

Imagine a writer who has had an idea for a novel for years but has always been limited by time and resources. With generative AI, she can use tools like ChatGPT to develop complex dialogues and elaborate plots in minutes or simply seek inspiration during creative droughts. Now, her vision can materialize faster and more accurately than she ever imagined. This not only speeds up the creative process but also allows creators to explore multiple ideas and iterations without the fear of wasting resources. I like to think of these tools as part of the creative process, not the final creators. I love starting to explore an idea and realizing along the way the endless possibilities of that idea, then narrowing it down to what works best for the concept I want to tell. The story is always the focus. "Generative AI can democratize the creation of high-quality audiovisual content, allowing small creators to compete with major studios by lowering the barriers of technical expertise and cost." (Valenzuela, 2022, p. 34).

Visual artists also benefit enormously from these technologies. A digital painter can use Midjourney to experiment with styles and techniques that would otherwise take years to master. AI can suggest combinations of colors, textures, and shapes that the artist might not have considered, taking their work to new heights. The journey is as important as the destination itself.

5.3.5 Generative AI and Audiovisual Narrative

Generative AI is not only transforming the process of creating images and text, but it is also revolutionizing audiovisual narrative. Films, series, and video games are entering a new era of creativity, where creators can experiment with stories and visual styles without traditional limitations. "Tools like Runway, Midjourney, and others are not just assisting creators, they are partners in the creative process, augmenting human creativity with the power of computation." (Altman, 2022).

Consider the case of an independent filmmaker who dreams of making a science fiction epic. Previously, this would have required an astronomical budget and a team of hundreds. Now, with tools like Runway, Magnific, and Midjourney, this filmmaker can generate impressive visual effects and build detailed worlds at a fraction of the cost and time. We may not yet be at the point where we can create a movie like Alien entirely with AI, but we are getting closer. In any case, it's not necessary for AI to generate the entire film; the important thing is that it can help create backgrounds, storyboards, character creation, mood boards, or concepts for the art department. It can help with the soundtrack or a part of the script that has you blocked.

5.3.6 *The Dawn of a New Era*

AI did not burst into our lives like a storm; rather, it was like the slow but inexorable advance of the tide. Initially, it was a novelty, an auxiliary tool that helped us with mundane tasks. But as algorithms became more sophisticated, we began to glimpse their true potential. In the audiovisual industry, this evolution has been particularly impactful. It feels both fast and slow. The videos we saw in 2023 of Will Smith eating spaghetti were laughable. The results in 2024 from platforms like Sora, Luma, or Runway are of a realism that excites many and scares others. For example, I recommend watching the short film Air Head by Shy Kids. The first short film made with Sora that truly set a precedent, showing that it is possible to create pieces with story and realism using AI. I had the pleasure of interviewing them on my YouTube channel, and it was very interesting to hear about their creative process, the difficulties they faced using AI, and their perspective.

Imagine a summer afternoon in a small film studio. Creators are immersed in their computers, not just editing sequences but conversing with artificial intelligences that understand their needs and anticipate their desires. This is not science fiction; it is our new reality. AI allows independent filmmakers to compete with major studios, democratizing access to tools that were once exclusive to a privileged elite.

This revolution is not only redefining how we create content but also how we consume it. Today's audiences are not just looking for entertainment; they crave immersive experiences that transport them to new worlds. AI is making these experiences possible, allowing creators to design narratives that are so realistic and immersive that the lines between fiction and reality fade.

In this new era, the true beneficiaries are those with an innate passion for storytelling. Artists, creators, and storytellers find in AI a powerful ally that amplifies their creative capacities. However, this change also brings significant challenges. Technicians and professionals who were once indispensable may find their skills replaced by faster and more precise algorithms. This phenomenon is not new; every industrial revolution has seen the disappearance of certain jobs and the creation of others. The key lies in adaptability and the willingness to learn new skills.

AI is not here to eliminate human creativity; it is here to enhance it. But this new reality also demands a high degree of responsibility and ethics. We must be aware of the impact of our works and use AI in a way that enriches rather than distorts reality.

Imagine a television series created almost entirely by a single individual, using AI to generate scripts, design settings, animate characters, and edit the final product. This level of creative autonomy was unthinkable just a decade ago, but today it is within reach thanks to generative AI tools. This not only democratizes content creation but also opens the door to an explosion of diversity and originality in the stories being told.

5.3.7 Tools and Techniques

One of the reasons why generative AI is having such a profound impact is the variety and accessibility of available tools. Anyone who has used Photoshop or After Effects knows that the learning curve is quite steep. With these new platforms, achieving more or less interesting results is relatively quick in comparison. Some can even use your phone from the comfort of the sofa to create images or videos that are useful in small productions. Here are some of the most notable:

- **ChatGPT:** Capable of generating coherent and natural text, it is ideal for scripts, dialogues, and plot development. Creators can interact with the model to refine details and explore different narrative directions.
- **Midjourney:** An image generation tool that allows artists to create stunning visuals from textual descriptions. It is useful for storyboards, setting design, and conceptual art. I have used it extensively for creating images that I then animate for concepts or even music videos. It is very useful in the fashion world.
- **Runway:** Provides AI-powered video editing tools that can perform complex tasks such as video creation, object removal, visual style changes, and character animation. This streamlines the post-production process and allows creators to focus more on the narrative. It is one of the most beloved platforms by the community as it is designed for creators.
- **Suno:** Generates original music from user-defined parameters. It is ideal for filmmakers who need custom soundtracks without costly licensing restrictions. It is also great for having fun creating music from nonsensical lyrics. Beavis and Butt-Head would have had a blast using it.
- **Magnific:** Offers AI models for image quality enhancement, which is particularly useful in restoring old material or improving content captured in suboptimal conditions. It is amazing to see how your creation improves with an enhance and upscale. It also includes relight, which allows you to completely change the visual look of the image.
- **Freepik:** What started as an image bank has become one of the largest generative AI platforms. It is ideal for creating images at the speed of thought in different

styles. They are constantly developing their tools, allowing you to do inpaintings, style changes, upscaling …

These tools not only make the creation process more efficient but also allow creators to experiment and take risks in ways that were previously impossible due to time and budget constraints. The ability to iterate quickly means that creators can explore more ideas and refine their projects until they reach their desired vision.

5.3.8 *The Future of Creativity*

Generative AI is in its infancy, and we are already seeing a significant impact on the audiovisual industry. As technology advances, we can expect tools to become even more sophisticated and accessible. In fact, what we see today is the worst we will ever see in AI. This will allow for unprecedented creativity, where technical barriers disappear, leaving only the creator's imagination.

The future promises an even closer collaboration between humans and machines. AI will become a natural extension of our creativity, allowing us to realize our visions with unmatched precision and efficiency. The stories we have always wanted to tell but seemed out of reach can now become reality. Something that excites me is that people who never had access to the necessary tools to tell their stories or realize their visions can now create authentic works of art thanks to access to the internet and generative AI platforms. Prepare for an explosion of unprecedented creativity.

Moreover, the integration of AI into the creative process has the potential to change how we value and consume art. In a world where anyone can create high-quality content, authenticity and originality will become the main differentiators. Creators who can infuse their works with a unique vision and an authentic voice will be the ones who stand out the most.

5.4 Conclusions

The AI revolution in the audiovisual industry is an inescapable reality. Although it brings significant challenges, it also offers unprecedented opportunities for those willing to adapt and take advantage of these new tools. Human creativity, with its inherent need to create, will remain the primary driver of this revolution. Let's prepare to ride this technological wave, using AI to enhance our imagination and expand the limits of what is possible in audiovisual creation.

AI is not the enemy; it is a powerful tool that, when used well, can transform the way we see and understand the world. Although I honestly prefer not to judge it because, like it or not, it is here to stay. We are at a point where we either adapt or step aside. As with any revolution, there will be those who resist change and those who embrace it. History has taught us that those who adapt are the ones who survive and thrive. And now, I leave you with some questions to ponder: Does AI scare you or excite you? What will change the most because of AI? Do you think we will be able to believe everything we see from now on? In fact, are you sure I wrote this text and not AI?

References

Altman, S. (2022). Generative AI and its role in modern creativity. *Advances in Artificial Intelligence, 17*(5), 88–104.

Johnson, A., & Lewis, P. (2020). Collaboration between AI and human creativity. *Creative Industries Journal, 12*(1), 20–35.

Roberts, C., Evans, M., & Harper, S. (2019). AI in creative workflows: Blurring boundaries. *Journal of Creative Technology, 15*(4), 98–110.

Smith, J. (2021). Artificial intelligence and the audiovisual industry: New frontiers of creativity. *Journal of Digital Media, 8*(3), 45–67.

Valenzuela, C. (2022). The democratization of content creation through AI. *Digital Arts Review, 9*(2), 30–45.

Jesús Plaza is a renowned Film & Creative Director, with experience ranging from conceptualization to the direction of fiction and advertising. He has led international teams and significantly contributed to the growth of the audiovisual industry with his innovative and creative approach. Additionally, he is a passionate explorer and advocate of Generative AI, having created numerous pieces utilizing these technologies. His work not only stands out for its technical quality but also for his ability to integrate AI into creative processes, offering a fresh and avant-garde vision of the future of art and technology. For him, the most important thing is to keep the focus on the story you want to tell; the rest are tools to tell it. Among his international recognitions are a Shortlist at the Berlin Fashion Film Festival for his work "Waves" and the Best Short Film award at Plasencia en Corto, a festival preselector for the Goya Awards, for his short film "Birdie." Since 2024, he has also been working with Sony Pictures Spain as an Audio Visual Content Manager, consolidating his role as an audiovisual innovator.

Chapter 6
Ethical and Legal Challenges of Artificial Intelligence with Respect to Intellectual Property

Patricia Lalanda and Neus Alcolea Roig

6.1 Introduction

Artificial Intelligence (AI) is transforming society and offering significant advancements across various sectors. However, its rapid development raises critical ethical and legal concerns, particularly regarding civil rights European Commission (2023). AIs are increasingly utilized in content generation at an unparalleled magnitude, introducing a new challenge in the realm of intellectual property (IP) law. This chapter delves into the intricate intersection between AI technology and IP rights, taking especially into account the Authors' home country legislation, Spain. It explores the challenges and opportunities arising from AI in the realm of IP protection, analyzing concerns such as authorship attribution, ownership of AI-generated works, and the influence of AI on IP regulations and frameworks highlighting the need for robust legal frameworks and ethical guidelines to ensure these innovations respect and protect civil rights. As AI continues its evolution, it becomes increasingly critical to address these challenges meticulously in order to maintain a delicate equilibrium between technological advancement and the preservation of essential human values European Parlimentary Research Service. (2020).

Moreover, relevant jurisdictions will be analyzed, notably the United States, China, and the European Union (UE), in order to gain insights into how significant global powers that leverage AI are addressing this crucial issue, in contrast to the European Union, which serves as another regulatory cornerstone, similar to its precedent with data protection regulations, extending its jurisdiction beyond EU borders with a commitment to safeguarding, ensuring security, and acting as a guarantor of the fundamental rights of its residing citizens.

P. Lalanda (✉) · N. A. Roig
Loyra Abogados (Law Firm), Intellectual Property, Entertainment, Data Protection, New Technologies and AI, Madrid, Spain
e-mail: patricia.lalanda@loyra.com; neus.alcolea@loyra.com

A. Baraybar-Fernández et al. (eds.), *The AI Revolution*, Research Series on Responsible Enterprise Ecosystems, https://doi.org/10.1007/978-3-031-80411-3_6

6.2 Intellectual Property

6.2.1 AI's Impact on Intellectual Property Rights

In science fiction stories, AI is a threat to the physical integrity of humanity. However, since the qualitative leap of AI due to generative intelligence, one of the major concerns of humans has been and continues to be the impact of AI on intangible intellectual property assets. This is because generative AI can create these assets faster and cheaper than humans. Therefore, certain questions arise from the problems that result from the use of AI in our lives and specifically in creative processes. Among them, those that are particularly more interesting: Can the creation of an AI be considered a work protected by IP rights? And if so, who holds ownership rights over creations generated by AI?

Before addressing these issues, one must pause and ponder whether content generated by AI qualifies as intellectual property warranting legal protection.

Therefore, a variety of questions arise:

6.2.2 Can the Creation of an AI Be Considered a Work Subject to IP Right?

To do so, it must fit the definition of the applicable regulations.

The Berne Convention,[1] to which 181 countries are members;[2] such as: the United States of America, most of European countries—Spain, France, Italy, Germany, United Kingdom Japan, Australia, among others—states in article 2 the definition and consideration of what are "Protected Works":

> (1) The expression 'literary and artistic works' shall include every production in the literary, scientific and artistic domain, whatever may be the mode or form of its expression.

Such definition is very similar to the Royal Legislative Decree 1/1996, of April 12, 1996, approving the revised text of the Intellectual Property Law, regularizing, clarifying, and harmonizing the legal provisions in force on the subject ("Spanish IP Law"), stated in article 10.1. Said definition is very similar to other European regulations of continental legislation, which defines the works protected by said law as:

> all **original** literary, artistic or scientific creations **expressed by any means or medium**, tangible and intangible, now known or to be invented in the future

[1] The Berne Convention for the Protection of Literary and Artistic Works, known as the Berne Convention, is an international agreement that protects copyright. This convention was first adopted in 1886 in Berne, Switzerland, and sets minimum standards for copyright protection that all member countries must adhere to. It ensures that authors of literary and artistic works have certain rights over their creations, regardless of the country where these works are published.

[2] As of June 2024.

Consequently, for a creation to qualify for protection, it must exhibit originality and be expressible in any medium, whether existing presently or developed in the future. Thus, an endless number of creations may be considered protectable works as long as they are original. In this sense, both the Spanish IP Law and the Berne Convention describe a series of works that are considered protected works under said norms. However, it is important to note that this list is not considered *numerus clausus* by case law. That is precisely so that works that the legislator may have forgotten or do not exist yet are able to fit in said description. In this sense the Spanish IP Law states Real Decreto Legislativo (1996) (as do most of the world's regulations) specifically the following:

currently unknown or that may be invented in the future

The main point of conflict in relation to the content generated by AI lies in the term "original," from which another question arises: What is considered original? What is originality?

Jurisprudence categorizes originality into objective and subjective components:

1. *Objective:* the objective component encompasses absolute novelty, "uniqueness," individuality, and distinctiveness of the work.
2. *Subjective:* the subjective component encompasses free and creative decisions of the author (Case Cofemel—C-683/17) Judgement of the CJEU Cofemel 2019. The prevailing legal argument asserts that artificial intelligence has produced an array of new or original works, encompassing paintings, music, literature, poetry, and more, depending on the perspective adopted. Hence, when AI generates a work, it inherently qualifies as a work in principle. Consequently, the output of AI is regarded as copyrightable, even if the AI's creation process involves learning from existing human works, akin to how humans acquire knowledge. Essentially, AI assimilates knowledge from past works similar to human learning to innovate and produce new creations. Nonetheless, a minority view contends that originality in AI creations is debatable due to their reliance on external sources, although this argument parallels human creativity. This debate is based precisely on the fact that AI operates with a learning system based on humans' creations, therefore (i) it does not create on sole merit—but as we previously stated this argument pales in relation to the fact that AI learn as humans—(ii) and learns (trains) with works that hold intellectual property rights form third parties.

In conclusion, the works generated by AI may be eligible for legal protection; however, the identification of the author and rightful owner of authorship remains uncertain. Legally speaking, this concept lacks a final definition.

6.2.3 Can AI Systems Be Considered Authors and Therefore Be Holders of Intellectual Property Rights?

There are four potential authors of a work generated through the use of AI:

1. The AI system
2. The developer of the AI
3. The individual providing instructions to the AI or initiating the creation process (by activating the "Create" function or performing the legal "generative act")
4. A collaboration between 2 and 3 above.

The term "authorship" lacks a precise legal definition. While the Berne Convention does not explicitly outline the concept of authorship, it emphasizes the paramount importance of safeguarding the rights of human individuals in the creative process. It must be noted that the European Union has not established a unified normative framework or directives to standardize the definition of "authorship."

The Spanish IP Law Real Decreto Legislativo (1996) establishes that IP protect: "the author, who is the one who performs the purely human and personal task of creation of the work and who, therefore, constitutes the essential core of the object of this Law." In the phrase "the purely human task," it is evident, explicit, and unequivocal that authorship pertains strictly and exclusively to the human beings by their very nature. They alone are capable of creating works. The term "personal" underlines the necessity for human authors to engage in the creative process, further implying the essential element of originality. It is evident in the governing legislations that to be recognized as an author, the work must originate from the creativity of a human being. This concept is encapsulated by the French perspective, describing works created by authors as "works of the spirit," where a part of the creator's essence is believed to be imbued within the creation.

Thus, can AI be considered the author and therefore hold authorship? It is essential to examine the two fundamental requirements of authorship to determine if this is feasible:

1. The author must be a legal person, whether a natural person or a corporate entity.
2. The creation must qualify as a work of authorship, meaning it must be original and not merely a product of a technical process.

The first requirement does not currently apply to AI systems, as they lack legal entity. However, many intellectual property regulations include provisions for exceptional circumstances in which a legal entity may hold copyright. This raises the question of whether an exception could be made for AI, allowing it to be recognized as a legal entity capable of holding rights to a work. This argument ultimately hinges on the willingness of regulators to create such an exception within the applicable legal framework.

The second requirement is more determinative because it relies on pre-existing criteria for considering a creation as a work of authorship. This suggests that in cases where AI is not recognized as the author, a third party who meets the criteria for authorship can assert ownership of the work. This evaluation is contingent upon the originality and creative contribution during the creation process, guaranteeing that the work is not solely a product of technical operations.

Disregarding the second criterion for the moment, as it has already been addressed in Section 1, we now turn to determining the second criterion for this purpose, two cases are analyzed:

1. The case of the primate Naruto (see Fig. 6.1), who in 2011 took some photos of itself. Although it took the photographs in an autonomous and independent way, Naruto holds no legal personality, and therefore cannot hold ownership of IP property—or any property—therefore cannot be considered the author of the pictures. The author was determined by the US judge to be the human photographer, who prearranged and prepared the camera waiting for a reaction from the primate.
2. CJEU ruling Painer case C-145/10 Judgement of the ECOJ (2011): The CJEU states that "the photographer may choose between various developing or printing techniques, or, where necessary, apply computer software" and this does not mean that the work belongs to the technical element that allowed the realization. This highlights the necessity for the author of an original work to have made individual creative decisions during the creation process.

In this context, the CJEU ruling in Case Cofemel-C-683/1 Judgement of the CJEU Cofemel (2019) references the necessity of "free and creative decisions," along with a recognizable expression of personality attributable to the author. The case originated from a dispute in Portugal involving G-Star Raw CV and Cofemel—Sociedade de Vestuário SA on whether certain clothing designs, by G-Star Raw CV,

Fig. 6.1 Naruto selfie. Source: Wikimedia Commons. / © David Slater: Wildlife Personalities Ltd

should be protected by copyright as original works of art. The Portuguese courts referred the case to the CJEU to clarify the interpretation of EU copyright law, particularly regarding the requirement of originality. The CJEU ruled that copyright protection extends to any original work created by an author's own intellectual creation. The decision emphasized that the artistic or aesthetic value of the work is not a determining factor for copyright eligibility. Instead, what matters is whether the work reflects the author's creative choices and expresses their personality. As described in the ruling, it is evident that there is no concept of personality in the legal context for the author. This observation could potentially suggest that AI, which possesses the ability to autonomously make decisions, may exhibit such personality traits. The autonomy and decision-making capability demonstrated by AI align precisely with the assertions made by the European Group on Ethics in Science and New Technologies.

In assessing the significance of the authorship definition, it is argued that an author should possess creative autonomy, allowing them the liberty to make independent decisions. Nonetheless, this definition may not be universally applicable, as it is crucial to recognize that the intent to create holds greater importance than a strict interpretation of free and spontaneous will. In such scenarios, a creator hired to write a script in exchange for payment may not be deemed to act out of their own volition, given that the impetus comes from an external source, potentially disqualifying them as an author due to the absence of creative autonomy. Conversely, AI, although instructed on tasks, possesses the capacity to determine and delineate its executions and presentations through its neural network, thereby warranting a broad consideration of autonomy.

As previously indicated, one potential solution could involve endowing AI with a legal fiction, analogous to the corporate entities with legal personality, thus creating a digital persona capable of asserting rights. However, the current stance of the EU leans toward prioritizing the protection of human individuals, making the incorporation of such a concept into our legal framework a complex endeavor.

In the context of the CJEU ruling on the Brompton case—C-833/18, the concept of free and creative decisions that contribute originality to a work subjectively excludes decisions influenced by the technical constraints of the creation process.

In short, to understand that the AI can be an author, it should reflect its creativity and autonomous decisions in the work Judgement of the ECOJ (2011). Since it acts analogously to a human brain and when it initiates its creation, it is the one that makes the cognitive and therefore creative process of the work, it could be considered that it chooses its own creative processes to realize the work. And, therefore, the AI could be considered an author by these terms. However, this would not be appropriate in relation to what the spirit of most of the laws that defend intellectual property want to defend, that is the humanistic component of the creation of the work.

As per the other two other contenders for authorship, the developer of the AI and the individual providing instructions, often referred to as "prompts," to the AI or initiating the creation process, both options could potentially be regarded as authors, given their legal characteristics, but the determination hinges on whether they genuinely contribute to the creation of the work; The determination of authorship varies case by case, contingent upon: (i) If the AI's creator programs it for autonomous work generation, as exemplified by projects like "The Next Rembrandt"[3] the creator of the AI becomes the author and (ii) Conversely, in cases where the user not only activates the AI but also dictates the work's specifics, as seen in scenarios like the "Medley[4]", the user of the AI might be recognized as a creator.

Regarding the authorship as a collaboration between the creator of the IA and the one who uses it, many legal systems define a category known as "collaborative work." In practice, collaborative works are typically understood to be those created by two or more authors who contribute to the creation of a single work. Each contributor retains rights in the part of the work they have created, while joint rights are commonly shared over the entire work. This interpretation is consistent with the underlying principles of the Berne Convention, despite the treaty not expressly delineating the term "collaborative work."

The specific definition and treatment of collaborative works are generally addressed in national copyright laws. Regarding this definition, the Spanish Intellectual Property Law states in Article 7, establishes that:

> The rights to a work that arises from the collaborative efforts of multiple authors are deemed to be collectively owned by all contributors.

In addition to the points raised above, there exists a clear reliance of AI on human individuals in the creative process, as AI lacks will and initiative. The AI is dependent on the individual who initiates the creation process by activating it and providing instructions. Consequently, if certain jurisdictions were to grant ownership rights of works to AI, a potential solution to uphold a human-centered perspective could involve categorizing works created by AI as collaborative efforts. This approach would serve when the AI has been the primary creator of the work rather than merely a tool or assistant in the creation process. By considering the work as a collaborative endeavor, it would enable the natural person to benefit from the investment and creative input put into the AI.

Currently, and due to the legal uncertainty, these determinations are typically established through private agreements between the involved parties, be it contracts or terms and conditions. Hence, seeking guidance from legal and technical experts is paramount in navigating these complex issues effectively.

---

[3] A closed generative AI project in which the AI creates only for that purpose then we can conclude that the author is the creator of the AI. The creator of the AI is also the author since he has entered and used the AI for his art project.

[4] "Medley"is a case study that explores the integration of Generative AI—through ChatGPT and Midjourney—into a reinvented version of Apple's yearly Replay.

6.2.4 Can the Intellectual Property Rights of Works Created by AI Be Deemed to Belong to the Public Domain?

It is suggested by some that the output created by AI could be deemed as part of the public domain mainly due to the fact that the creator of the AI already benefits economically from protecting and commercializing the AI as software. However, from a legal standpoint, this viewpoint oversimplifies the matter. The concept of the public domain exists to preserve and promote cultural heritage, signifying that releasing intellectual property rights is a measure in support of culture but does not impact the authorship title of the work. These are distinct concepts. Even works produced anonymously or under a pseudonym are granted intellectual property rights. If the output of AI is recognized as a work, it will be entitled to the same rights as any other creation.

6.2.5 Is It Plausible to Characterize Works Generated by AI as Plagiarism Due to Their Reliance on Existing Works for Inspiration?

Given the understanding that the current advancement of AI and their internal learning mechanisms relies heavily on accessing copyrighted works, it leads us to ponder whether the creations emanating from AI could be considered plagiarism.

In reality, assessing whether the work generated by AI qualifies as plagiarism hinges on the existing regulations and established legal precedents that define what constitutes plagiarism. This nuanced evaluation often requires the proficiency of an expert witness, considering that human creators similarly draw inspiration and knowledge from external sources. Therefore, despite the advanced capabilities of AI, including its vast memory, access to extensive datasets, high processing speeds, and cost-effectiveness, it may not be prudent to categorically label AI-generated work as plagiarism.

6.2.6 Can One Utilize the Work Created Through an AI?

When utilizing AI programs, considerations regarding the data utilized by the platform, confidentiality, terms and conditions, and adherence to legal frameworks come into play. Existing regulations, although not exclusive to AI, are applicable. Specific regulations including trade secrets, trademark law, patents, data protection, intellectual property, supplier contracts, and terms and conditions are relevant and must be taken into consideration. It is important to establish contractual regulations for AI creations in the absence of specific legal guidelines.

At an ethical level, it is recommended to utilize AI not as an end in itself but as a tool that supplements work and creation, serving as a technical component facilitating realization. It's important to recognize the potential benefits of technological advancement and avoid falling behind, given its utility across various aspects of life, including not just creation but also in domains like healthcare, finance, technology, and others.

6.3 Immersion in Comparative Law

When analyzing a complex and fairly new matter such as the regulation of AI and its implications with respect to legal rights such as IP rights, it is essential to delve into how various jurisdictions are approaching it in order to gain a broader perspective and enhance the legal reasoning. Around the globe, countries are formulating and implementing AI governance legislation to match the rapid and varied growth of AI-powered technologies. These legislative efforts involve the creation of voluntary guidelines and standards, specific regulations for particular use cases, and comprehensive laws.

While these individual jurisdictions advance with their own approaches, based on their legal frameworks, opportunity policies and social values, multilateral efforts to coordinate AI regulative approach intensify. The priority of these is to achieve a strict balance between the potential risks associated with AI systems and the risk of losing the economic and social benefits that the new technology can bring to the table.

6.3.1 United States: Regulatory Approaches, and Strategies for the Development of AI

The US government is committed to a global action that they must lead, regarding AI technology as its regulation Biden Administration. (2023).

As the tangible capabilities of the technology materialized rapidly over the years, the US government acknowledged the far-reaching potential for interdisciplinary applications and the significant associated risks. Regulatory emphasis has shifted toward the control of these capabilities in significantly risky scenarios.

While the US and European visions of AI inherent risks are largely aligned, US legal action addressing those risks is not currently enforceable and has more of a declaratory nature.

The initial regulatory approach from 2016 to 2020 was driven toward fostering innovation and promoting research and development. During this period, there was minimal policy control over technology, reflecting a more *laissez-faire* stance. The strategy employed was primarily programmatic.

The overall approach of the US aims to achieve global leadership in AI technologies through cutting-edge innovation. It seeks to set a worldwide example for responsible AI regulation, emphasizing excellence over trust. The primary focus of the regulatory framework is to promote competitiveness and mitigate risks that threaten innovation, rather than imposing limitations and restrictions for enhanced control. There is a strong emphasis on corporate governance and best practices. The implementation of laws and executive policies relies on a complex framework of federal agencies. The approach focuses on targeted risk regulations specific to particular AI sectors, with significant concerns about national security risks and economic risks, such as workforce implications. Societal perceived risks include harmful AI, discrimination, privacy protection, and copyright issues. The following are the AI US initiative objectives that are summarized in the following table provided by USPTO[5] (Fig. 6.2).

Lastly, the Biden Government approved a Blueprint for an AI Bill of Rights White House Office of Science and Technology Policy. (2022), a white paper consisting of a set of five principles and associated practices to help guide the design, use, and deployment of automated systems to protect citizens' rights in the age of AI. However, neither this document nor any other of legal nature has solved the issue of movie scripts and AI in the United States, one of the most conflicting issues in this respect to date; Within 6 months of the release of ChatGPT, generative artificial intelligence had already sparked widespread unease throughout Hollywood. One of the primary concerns was the potential for chatbots to write or rewrite scripts, leading TV and film screenwriters to strike at the beginning of 2023. This issue was addressed in the 2023 SAG-AFTRA TV/Theatrical Agreement, which outlines specific protections for writers and establishes guidelines for the use of AI in scriptwriting, effectively bringing resolution to the industry's apprehensions, at least for the moment.

Fig. 6.2 Main objectives of the initial US National AI Initiative. Source: USTPO (United States Patent and Trademark Office)

[5] United States Patent and Trademark Office, USPTO.

6.3.2 China: Regulatory Framework, Implementation Strategies, Enforcement Issues

From an R&D[6] perspective, the race for research, industrial, and market leadership has been for years between China and the United States. Yet in the legal sphere, all three blocks (including the EU, discussed below) claim to be the first regulators, with the aim of setting an influential precedent. Ultimately, however, which approach proves to be future-proof and adapts best to technological and social developments will be the decisive factor.

China is committed to a long-distance race for cutting-edge innovation, combining the efforts of the public sector and the domestic economy. Therefore, China's approach to AI regulation is characterized by a combination of strategic planning, strict oversight, and an emphasis on both technological innovation and social stability Yong, W. (2021).

Said strategic planning aims at making the country a global AI leader by 2030 Yang, Z. (2024). It emphasizes centralized control through government oversight and the implementation of stringent data security and privacy laws. Ethical guidelines promote responsible AI use, focusing on public welfare and mitigating social impacts. China supports technological innovation with substantial R&D investment and promotes international collaboration while ensuring technological sovereignty.

Therefore, launched in 2017, China's "Next Generation Artificial Intelligence Development Plan" sets out the following main highlights (see Fig. 6.3):

1. **Centralized Control**: The Chinese government maintains strict control over AI development and deployment. This includes setting national standards, issuing guidelines, and implementing policies that align with broader national objectives.

2020	2025	2030
• Develop the next generation of AI technologies on big data, swarm intelligence, hybrid enhanced intelligence and autonomous intelligence systems	• Make AI the primary driver for China's industrial advances and economic transformation	• Become the world's premier AI innovation centre
• Gather the world's leading AI talents together	• Use AI in a wide range of fields – manufacturing, medicine, national defence	• Develop major breakthroughs in research and development
• Establish initial frameworks for AI laws, regulations, ethics and policy	• Become a leading player in AI research and development	• Expand the use of AI through social governance and national defence
	• Finalise AI laws, regulations, ethical norms, policies and safety mechanisms	• Create leading AI innovation and personnel training bases

Fig. 6.3 Main goals of Chinese Artificial Intelligence Strategy for the 2020 decade. Source: 'The Age of Artificial Intelligence, Towards a European Strategy for Human- Centric Machines', EPSC, 2018

[6] Promotion of Research and Development (R&D).

2. **Regulatory Bodies**: Various government agencies, such as the Ministry of Industry and Information Technology and the Cyberspace Administration of China, play crucial roles in overseeing AI regulations, ensuring compliance, and promoting ethical standards.
3. **Ethical Guidelines**: China has introduced guidelines to promote the ethical use of AI, focusing on issues such as privacy protection, data security, and the prevention of algorithmic bias. These guidelines aim to balance technological innovation with social responsibility.

A notable case of AI-generated intellectual property in China was "Xiaomingbot," an AI developed by Microsoft and Beijing University, which published a collection of poems titled "The Sunlight That Lost the Glass Window" in 2017. The Chinese government has responded proactively to such advancements, investing heavily in AI research and infrastructure as part of its strategic plan to become a global leader in AI by 2030. Additionally, the government has been updating its intellectual property laws to address challenges posed by AI-generated content, wanting to ensure clarity on ownership and rights, this matter is still a topic of debate, but for the time being all indications point to the conclusion that only natural persons and legal entities will be entitled to title to works that generate intellectual property rights.

These updates include defining the ownership of AI-generated works, determining the legal rights and responsibilities of AI developers and users, and establishing guidelines for attributing AI-generated content. The Chinese government also prioritizes aligning AI development with societal values and ethical standards, promoting public awareness and education to balance innovation with the protection of human creators' interests.

6.3.3 Scope of the EU AI Act: Key Provisions, Extraterritorial Application, Compliance Requirements, Safeguarding Fundamental Rights, Technological and Legal Safeguards

The EU is committed to ethical values, fundamental rights protection and transparency, intending long-term confidence of users and citizens European Commission. (2024). The EU advocates for a harmonized practical risk-based framework. One notable aspect of this legislation is its extraterritorial reach, meaning that its regulations and restrictions extend beyond the borders of the European Union. This implies that companies and organizations based outside the EU that provide AI products or services to EU residents will also be subject to compliance with the regulations outlined in the AI Act. This move toward extraterritorial enforcement signifies the EU's commitment to ensuring the responsible and ethical deployment of AI technologies, even when developed or operated by entities located outside its jurisdiction. By extending its regulatory authority in this manner, the EU aims to safeguard individuals within its borders and uphold standards of transparency, accountability, and data protection in the field of artificial intelligence European Council of the EU (2024).

The European Union is navigating the complex landscape of digital risks with a new strategy that emphasizes the creation of reliable, ethical, and anthropocentric AI, distinguishing itself from the approaches taken by the United States and Russia/China European Parliment. (2023).

In regard to the Digital risks, as AI technologies advance, so do the associated risks, including privacy breaches, security threats, and ethical concerns. Addressing these digital risks is paramount to fostering public trust and ensuring the responsible deployment of AI. The "AI made in the EU" approach is focused as a benchmark for reliability, ethics, and human-centered development. This approach contrasts with the more laissez-faire attitude of the US and the more state-controlled methods observed in Russia and China. By focusing on stringent ethical standards and the protection of fundamental rights, the EU seeks to create a unique and trustworthy AI ecosystem.

(a) **Scope of the EU AI Act Future of Life Institute (2024)**

On March 13, 2024, the EU introduced the EU Regulation AI (AI Act), a significant legislative measure designed to regulate AI within its jurisdiction. This regulation builds on the foundation laid by the General Data Protection Regulation (GDPR) and aims to enhance security and promote a unified single market for AI technologies.

(b) **Key Elements of the EU AI Act**

i. Objective: The primary goals are to ensure security and facilitate a single market for AI, providing a cohesive regulatory environment across member states.

ii. Regulation Framework: The AI Act establishes a harmonized framework, offering a minimum set of safety standards while allowing for complementary regulations. This ensures that AI systems are developed safely without stifling innovation.

iii. Safety Safeguards: The regulation outlines ultimate safety safeguards, focusing on protection against risks rather than prescribing specific development methodologies for AI. This flexible approach allows innovation to flourish while maintaining rigorous safety standards.

iv. Content:

- Risk Categorization: AI systems are categorized based on the level of risk they pose, with specific prohibitions for high-risk applications (see Fig. 6.4).
- Transparency and Traceability: Requirements for transparency and traceability are imposed to ensure that AI systems can be audited and understood, promoting accountability.

v. Open Regulation: The AI Act is designed to be open and adaptive, with delegation acts that can be supplemented by additional rules. Regulation by

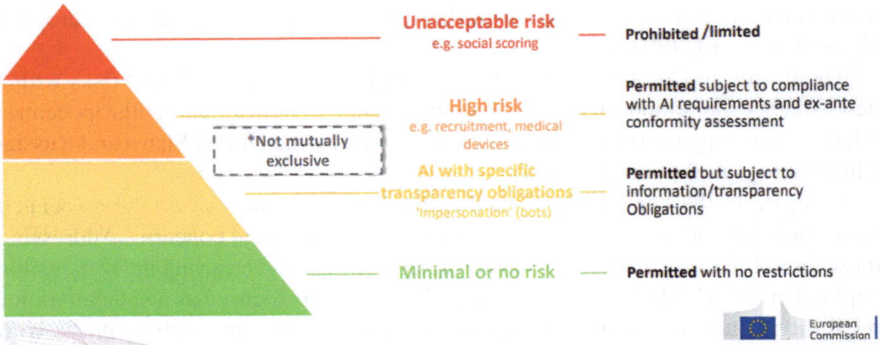

Fig. 6.4 Risk-level classification as defined by the European Artificial Intelligence Act. Source: 'Shaping Europe's Digital Future: A European Strategy AI', European Commission, 2021

principles, such as ensuring safety, allows the framework to evolve alongside technological advancements.

In summary, the EU's AI strategy, embodied in the AI Act, represents a deliberate effort to balance the need for technological innovation with the imperative to protect citizens' rights and ensure safety. By creating a reliable, ethical, and anthropocentric AI framework, the EU aims to set a global standard that differentiates its approach from that of other major powers, fostering a trustworthy and secure digital ecosystem.

In this regard, following the guidelines and willing of the European Union, the Spanish Government has released a guide of good practices regarding the use of artificial intelligence stating that they are not in favor, nor they would admit AI as a creator for public grants Culture Ministry (2024). In this context, Spain has established a regulatory sandbox under Royal Decree 817/2023, dated November 8, which creates a controlled testing environment for assessing compliance with the proposed EU Regulation on harmonized rules for artificial intelligence systems Real Decreto (2023) and Estrategia de Inteligencia Artificial 2024.

6.4 Conclusion

As we conclude the exploration of Artificial Intelligence's regulation and specifically the impact on intellectual property, it becomes evident that AI is fundamentally reshaping the landscape of creation, ownership, ethics, and economics within the creative industries. This transformation presents both opportunities and challenges that must be navigated with careful consideration. There is no cause for alarm. AI has the potential to serve as a valuable aid and creative tool for individuals in the future. It can assist artists in enhancing or actualizing their vision. Nevertheless, it is essential to recognize that AI does not independently create the work and that IP rights exist to protect the human creator. Therefore, AI merely functions as a tool that complements and supports the human creator. The main takeaways are the following:

(i) **AI as a Creation Tool**

AI technologies have significantly enhanced creative processes across various domains, from music and art to literature and design. These tools facilitate unprecedented levels of collaboration between humans and tools, enabling creators to push the boundaries of their craft. Legal recognition of AI's contributions is still evolving, with many jurisdictions grappling with how to attribute and protect works generated with substantial AI assistance.

(ii) **AI as a Creator**

Instances of AI-created works are becoming increasingly common, raising complex questions about ownership and attribution. Unlike traditional works created by human authors, AI-generated content challenges the existing intellectual property framework. Who owns a piece of art created entirely by an AI? Can an AI be considered an author? Legal precedents are gradually emerging, but a consensus is yet to be reached. These developments call for robust legal frameworks that can address the unique characteristics of AI-generated works while protecting the rights of human creators.

(iii) **Ethical Implications**

The rise of AI in creative fields brings forth ethical concerns, particularly regarding human displacement. As AI systems become more proficient in generating creative content, there is a legitimate fear of reduced demand for human creators. Additionally, the moral rights of human creators, such as the right to be recognized as the author of a work and to object to derogatory treatments of their creations, need to be safeguarded in an AI-driven world. Balancing the drive for innovation with the protection of human contributors is crucial to ensure a fair and ethical integration of AI into the creative process.

(iv) **Economic Implications**

AI's impact on creative industries is profound, influencing market dynamics and economic structures. While AI can democratize content creation and reduce production costs, it can also lead to market saturation and devaluation of creative works. Policymakers must address these economic shifts by implementing measures that support sustainable growth and fair competition. Recommendations include incentivizing innovation, providing support for displaced workers, and ensuring that AI advancements benefit the broader creative economy rather than concentrating power in the hands of a few.

In summary, the intersection of AI and intellectual property presents a multifaceted landscape that requires thoughtful consideration and proactive regulation. By acknowledging and addressing the legal, ethical, and economic implications of AI, we can harness its potential to enhance creativity while protecting the rights and livelihoods of human creators. As we move forward, a balanced approach that promotes innovation and safeguards intellectual property will be essential in shaping a future where AI and human creativity coexist harmoniously.

Acknowledgments The authors wish to acknowledge the contributions of several individuals and organizations to the completion of this chapter. Firstly, they extend their gratitude to Mr. Antonio

Baraybar-Fernández and Mr. Sandro Arrufat-Martín for entrusting us with this writing journey. The authors also appreciate Ms. Paz Alexandra Sánchez-Arjona Gómez-Rodulfo's constructive support. And, lastly, they acknowledge the team at Loyra Abogados for their dedication and encouragement.

References

Biden Administration. (2023). *Exec. Order No. 14110 on the safe, secure, and trustworthy development and use of artificial intelligence*. https://www.whitehouse.gov/briefing-room/statements-releases/2023/10/30/executive-order-on-the-safe-secure-and-trustworthy-development-and-use-of-artificial-intelligence/

«BOE» núm. 268, d. 9. (Ed.). (n.d.). Real Decreto 817/2023, de 8 de noviembre, que establece un entorno controlado de pruebas para el ensayo del cumplimiento de la propuesta de Reglamento del Parlamento Europeo y del Consejo por el que se establecen normas armonizadas en materia de inteligen. *Boletin Oficial del Estado, de 8 de noviembre de 2023*. Retrieved from https://www.boe.es/eli/es/rd/2023/11/08/817

Alexander Cuntz, C. F. (2024). *Economic research working paper: artifical intelligence and intellectual property: An economic perspective No. 77/2024*. World Intellectual Property Organization (WIPO).

Committe on Legal Affairs of the European Parliment. (2020). *Report - A9–0176/2020 on intellectual property rights for the development of artificial intelligence technologies.*. European Parliment.

Culture Ministry. (2024, February). *Nota Informativa sobre Buenas Prácticas relativas a la utilización de sistemas*. Retrieved from Secretaria de Estado de Cultura: https://www.cultura.gob.es/dam/jcr:469163cc-0fdf-4fe2-964f-d4815cde40b1/240219-nota-informativa-ia.pdf

European Commission. (2023, October). *Proposal for a Directive of the European Parliament and of the Council on adapting non-contractual civil liability rules to artificial intelligence (AI Liability Directive) (2023/10/13(COD))*. Retrieved from https://eur-lex.europa.eu/legal-content/ES/TXT/?uri=CELEX:52022PC0496

European Commission. (2024). *Shaping Europe's digital future*. Retrieved from www.digital-strategy.ec.europa.eu: https://digital-strategy.ec.europa.eu/en/policies/regulatory-framework-ai

European Council of the EU. (2024, May). Artificial intelligence (AI) act: Council gives final green light to the first worldwide rules on AI. *Press releases*. Retrieved from https://www.consilium.europa.eu/en/press/press-releases/2024/05/21/artificial-intelligence-ai-act-council-gives-final-green-light-to-the-first-worldwide-rules-on-ai/

European Parliament. (2024, March). Legislative Resolution on the proposal for a regulation of the EuropeanParliment and of the Council onlayingdown harmonised rules on artificial Intelligence (Artificial Intelligence Act) and amending certainUnion legislative acts. European Parliment. doi:P9_TA(2024)0138.

European Parliment. (2017, May). European Parliament resolution of 16 February 2017 with recommendations to the Commission on Civil Law Rules on Robotics. *Adopted resolution*. Strasbourg. doi:2015/2103(INL)

European Parliment. (2023, June). AI rules: what the European Parliament wants. (E. Parliment, Ed.) Retrieved June https://www.europarl.europa.eu/topics/en/article/20201015STO89417/ai-rules-what-the-european-parliament-wants, 2023.

European Parlimentary Research Service. (2020). *The ethics of artificial intelligence: Issues and initiatives*. Panel for the Future of Science and Technology. Retrieved from https://www.europarl.europa.eu/RegData/etudes/STUD/2020/634452/EPRS_STU(2020)634452_EN.pdf

Future of Life Institute. (2024, May). High-level summary of the AI Act. Retrieved from EU Artificial Intelligence Act: https://artificialintelligenceact.eu/high-level-summary/

Judgement of the CJEU Cofemel – Sociedade de Vestuário S.A./G-Star Raw CV, C-683/17 (Third Chamber of the European Court of Justice September 12, 2019).

Judgement of the ECOJ Eva-Maria Painer v Standard VerlagsGmbH and Others. Case C-145/10 (European Court of Justice December 1, 2011).

Ministerio para la Transformación Digital y de la Función Pública. (2024). *Estrategia de Inteligencia Artificial 2024.*

Real Decreto Legislativo 1/1996, de 12 de abril, por el que se aprueba el texto refundido de la Ley de Propiedad Intelectual, regularizando, aclarando y armonizando las disposiciones legales vigentes sobre la materia. (n.d.). *Boletín Oficial del Estado, de 12 de Abril de 1996.* Retrieved from https://www.boe.es/eli/es/rdlg/1996/04/12/1/con

The European Parliament, the Council and the Commission. (2000, December). Charter of Fundamental Rights of the European Union. (2000/C 364/01). *Official Journal of the European Communities.*

Verweij, D. A. (2017). *Sizing the prize: what's the real value of AI for your business and how can you capitalise?* PwC.

WIPO. (2020). *Intellectual property and frontier technologies.* Retrieved May 2024, from wipo.int: https://www.wipo.int/about-ip/en/frontier_technologies/

World Intellectual Property Organization (WIPO). (2019) *Artificial intelligence.* WIPO Technology Trends. Retrieved May 4, 2023, from https://www.wipo.int/edocs/pubdocs/en/wipo_pub_1055.pdf

World Intellectual Property Organization (WIPO). (1886). Berne Convention for the Protection of Literary and Artistic Works of September 9, 1886, completed at Paris on May 4, 1896, revised at Berlin on November 13, 1908, completed at Berne on March 20, 1914, revised at Rome on June 2, 1928, revised at Brussels on June 26, 1948, and revised at Stockholm on July 14, 1967. volume-828-I-11850-English.pdf

World Intellectual Property Organization WIPO. (2020). *Intellectual property and frontier technologies.* Retrieved May 2024, from WIPO: https://www.wipo.int/about-ip/en/frontier_technologies/

White House Office of Science and Technology Policy. (2022). *Blueprint for an AI bill of rights.* Executive Office of the President of the United States. https://www.whitehouse.gov/wp-content/uploads/2022/10/Blueprint-for-an-AI-Bill-of-Rights.pdf

Yang, Z. (2024, January 17). *Four things to know about China's new AI rules in 2024.* MIT Technology Review: The Download. https://www.technologyreview.com/2024/04/09/1091010/the-download-how-china-plans-to-regulate-ai/

Yong, W. (2021). Copyright protection for AI-generated outputs: The experience from China. *Computer Law & Security Review, 42*, 105581.

Patricia Lalanda is a Partner at LOYRA Abogados, a law firm based in Madrid, Spain, with over 42 years specializing in regulated and highly technological sectors with and international practice. Ms. Lalanda leads the Intellectual Property, New Technologies and Data Protection department. Her work revolves around the latest innovative products in new technologies. She is a speaker on subjects such as land-based and online gaming, Artificial Intelligence, blockchain, cryptocurrencies and e-sports at various educational centers such as Universidad Autónoma de Madrid, Universidad Complutense de Madrid, IE Business School and Fundación de Investigación para el Derecho y la Empresa ("FIDE"). She also participates in national and international conferences including specific Artificial Intelligence conferences such as The AI Revolution (Madrid 2024). She frequently publishes on regulatory developments and her opinions thereon. In 2015, Patricia was awarded the title of "40 Under 40 Emerging Leader" by the American Gaming Association (Global Gaming Business Magazine, November 2015, issue: Emerging Leaders). Patricia studied law at Universidad Carlos III de Madrid and completed a master's degree in Intellectual Property, Information Technology and NNTT at Universidad Autónoma de Madrid.

Neus Alcolea Roig is an associate at LOYRA Abogados in the Intellectual Property, New Technologies and Data Protection department. She is a lawyer specialized in the audiovisual industry and new technologies and AI; she graduated in Spanish Law from the Complutense University of Madrid and in French Law from the Sorbonne University of Paris, the same university where she developed her international and European legal profile and discovered intellectual property, which she would later complete with her training in Spain in the Master of Intellectual Property at ICADE. In addition to this, she has worked in the audiovisual and new technologies sector, both in specialized audiovisual law firms and in technology companies. In 2022 she took the ECAM Master in Executive Production to give better industry advice to the sector; in addition to always continue training in AI, a latent issue and of vital importance for its effect on the areas of companies and creators. She has been speaker at numerous specific Artificial Intelligence conferences such as Conecta Fiction & Entertainment and the AI Revolution.

Chapter 7
Artificial Intelligence and Communication: The Threat of *Deepfake* Images

Lucas Morales Domínguez, José Luis Zurita Andión, and Malgorzata Kolankowska

7.1 Introduction

On October 7, 2023, a raid by Hamas guerrillas into Israeli territory sparked an armed conflict that resulted in an invasion of Palestine to overthrow the fundamentalist government. As of now, Israel continues to advance in a military offensive that won't let up until the terrorist group surrenders or is completely wiped out. This situation has only intensified the global divide that started with Russia invading Ukraine on February 24, 2022, and there's no end in sight. Consequently, while some talk about an Eastern Axis led by Russia and including BRICS countries—Brazil, India, China, and South Africa—and some Muslim governments, figures like Russian Foreign Minister Sergey Lavrov refer to the "Collective West" (2023:106), meaning NATO and its non-member allies, including the invaded Ukraine.

In today's geopolitical context, where wars are fought with unmanned drones—even homemade ones costing a few hundred euros have proven useful for covert attacks or rear-area resupply—and cutting-edge electronic devices. The battlefield has expanded to include social media, where propaganda plays an undeniable role. The era of post-truth and continual questioning of reality involves abandoning some of the principles that have underpinned scientific progress (Cortés, 2019, p. 416), leading us to assert that in postmodernism, the only certainty is uncertainty

L. M. Domínguez (✉) · J. L. Z. Andión
Department of Communication Sciences and Social Work of University of La Laguna, Canarias, Spain
e-mail: lmoraldo@ull.edu.es; jlzurita@ull.edu.es

M. Kolankowska
Department of Journalism and Social Communication of the University of Wroclaw, Wroclaw, Poland
e-mail: malgorzata.kolakowska@uwr.edu.pl

A. Baraybar-Fernández et al. (eds.), *The AI Revolution*, Research Series on Responsible Enterprise Ecosystems, https://doi.org/10.1007/978-3-031-80411-3_7

(Manrique, 2016, p. 162). This resulting decline in critical thinking makes it easier for hoaxes, fake news, AI compositions, or deepfake images to pass as authentic. Indeed, the need to fact-check information has driven the emergence and growth of European fact-checking platforms such as Maldita.es, Newtral, Pagella Politica, Les Décodeurs, or BBC Reality Check (García & López, 2020), tasked with verifying data. Platforms like X (formerly Twitter) now include community notes clarifying when a post is false or contains out-of-context images or videos. The prevalence of such misinformation is such that it's no surprise *fake news* was chosen as the Oxford and Collins dictionaries' word of the year in 2017 (García & López, 2020, p. 238).

Despite having these tools, there are other factors influencing the spread of false information. For instance, the high political polarisation in the West means that when individuals encounter posts that align with their beliefs, people don't spend much time verifying the authenticity of the information (Cortés, 2019, p. 416). In this process of constructing collective identity, it's crucial to note that we're at a crossroads: while communicative units like memes, whose propaganda potential is well-established, are not perceived as real—their strength lies in their message rather than their visuals—AI compositions strive to mimic situations to alter their meaning. Next, we'll delve into both compositions, focusing on their differences.

7.2 Synthetic Images: Distinguishing Characteristics

Deepfakes are defined as "fully synthetic images created using generative models" (Abdullah et al., 2024, p. 2), representing a significant advancement in digital photo manipulation (Barrientos et al., 2024, p. 4). The refinement of computer techniques that enable their creation is supported by the development of more sophisticated algorithms, increased computing power, and access to vast amounts of data (Franganillo, 2023, p. 2), which are distributed "online through techniques such as deep learning or machine learning" (Gómez & Tamayo, 2023, p. 3). Their high level of imitation—the improvements in AI applications depend on how well computer programmers understand the human brain (Fernández, 2022, pp. 339–340)—has resulted in "detecting the authenticity of the images becoming a critical problem" (Niteesh et al., 2021, p. 1), making some synthetic images indistinguishable from real ones (Chalmers, 2022), especially those produced through Generative Adversarial Networks (GAN).

Deepfake images are closely tied to social media (Sádaba & Salaverría, 2023, p. 21), to the extent that their emergence, development, and current spread can only be understood through the widespread use of these digital communication channels (Jacobsen & Simpson, 2023), as well as the multiplier effect of platforms like WhatsApp and Telegram. The significance of social media lies in the fact that it "has become an essential tool in the latest century in building social networks, conveying various forms of ideas and aspirations, from social to political aspects" (Aminulloh et al., 2022, p. 344).

We could point out that deepfake images share some conceptual similarities with memes, which are communicative units defined as "an image superimposed with a text description and are used to express a range of ideas such as humour, embarrassment, hate, propaganda, and even more emotions" (Gundapu & Mamidi, 2022, p. 1). Both share "several characteristics that make them abundant and prominent online" (Sanchez, 2020, p. 9) and "are broadly understood as multimodal cultural artefacts, which are created, remixed and circulated by users across digital platforms" (Rogers & Giorgi, 2024, p. 74).

The primary similarity between deepfake images and memes is that, on occasion, there is intentionality behind their sharing on the Internet. If we focus on politics, it is known that "memes continue to be produced and disseminated so that more and more people are pushed into getting involved with political events" (Aminulloh et al., 2022, p. 348), placing this product squarely in the realm of propaganda. Regarding these digital compositions and their use in propaganda, we can note the following:

> Propaganda is a communication tool used to achieve specific goals by shaping people's perceptions and behaviours. With the rise of social media, propaganda has become more effective and diverse. Detecting and filtering out propaganda is crucial for maintaining order in the online community. Unlike earlier approaches that focused on single-text formats, our focus is on memes, a multimodal format for propaganda that is widely popular on social media. Understanding both the visual and textual aspects of memes is essential for the task of detecting propaganda, but it's challenging due to the complex blend of multimodal information (Chen et al., 2024, p. 36630).

Despite these similarities, memes are considered a "piece of culture, typically a joke" (Davison, 2012, p. 122), where "the information can be in the form of text, image, or multimodal" (Chen et al., 2023, p. 36632). The visuo-lingual nature of memes increases the number and complexity of the propaganda variables they can contain. These are classified into 22 types: loaded language; name calling or labelling; doubt; exaggeration or minimisation; appeal to fear or prejudices; slogans; whataboutism; flag-waving; misrepresentation of someone's position (straw man); causal oversimplification; appeal to authority; thought-terminating cliché; black-and-white fallacy or dictatorship; reductio ad Hitlerum; repetition; obfuscation, intentional vagueness or confusion; presenting irrelevant data (red herring); bandwagon; smears; glittering generalities (virtue); appeal to (strong) emotions; and transfer (Dimitrov et al., 2019, pp. 6606–6607).

The reality is that deepfake images do not include verbal elements, so their study does not require multimodal systems that combine words and images. By relying solely on the visual aspect, synthetic images have given new meaning to our perception of things, making it so that "virtual objects are real objects, and what goes on in virtual reality is truly real" (Chalmers, 2017, p. 309). This can become dangerous, especially considering that some people who are generating false content can use this technology to create deceptive narratives that spread quickly and reach massive audiences (Garriga et al., 2024, p. 180).

7.3 Social Challenges to Address

The popularity of synthetic images has raised some ethical concerns in the present (Fernández, 2023, p. 345). One of the most negative aspects of deepfake images is that they are used as tools incorporating artificial intelligence technology that allows for face-swapping in images and voice modification, making the files appear original, authentic, and real (Garriga et al., 2024, p. 176). This characteristic not only enables the falsification of reality for political purposes but has also led to the creation of pornographic material intended to harm or blackmail individuals (Cerdán & Padilla, 2019). Studying this issue is crucial, considering that 96% of AI-generated images are pornographic (Martínez, 2023, p. 97).

The ability to alter reality in this way has given a new dimension to the term revenge porn, "that refers to the abuse of rights in the form of nonconsensual intimate image dissemination" (Mania, 2024, p. 117), leading to what is known as deepfake porn, a term that originated in Reddit forums (Wang & Kim, 2022). The rise of this new pornographic variant, which targets women involved in politics or individuals in close circles, such as high school teachers (Ballester et al., 2023, p. 234), has prompted online platforms like the adult content *PornHub*, and *Reddit* itself, to ban or impose significant restrictions on these synthetic contents (Barrientos et al., 2024, p. 3). It's no wonder that this trend of superimposing victims' images onto the bodies of other women to simulate sexual scenes or pornographic content (Vega et al., 2024, p. 5) is considered by some authors as socio-digital violence against women.

We cannot forget that this is nothing but evidence that deepfakes are a counter-information attack (Barrientos et al., 2024, p. 12), despite many journalistic editors using AI to enhance their articles with images, including illustrations and photos (Garriga et al., 2024, p. 180). For example, focusing on the Ukrainian conflict reveals that there are clear signs of a complex set of plans orchestrated from the power centre in the Kremlin to develop large-scale disinformation campaigns involving significant human, material, and technological resources (Figueroa, 2024, p. 92). The concern behind such cases is that deepfakes undermine the credibility of audiovisual documents, primarily videos, as means of information or certification of facts, questioning their accuracy or generating misinformation risks (Bañuelos, 2020, p. 52). In the case of the Israel-Palestine conflict, several deepfakes can be found on the Internet encouraging sympathy for the region governed by Hamas (Image 7.1).

As a final objection to this technology, some authors dare to fantasise about an apocalyptic scenario drawn from science fiction: the rebellion of machines. By enabling computers to mimic human minds, it wouldn't be far-fetched to think that a superintelligent artificial could perceive humans as a threat to its purposes (Fernández, 2022, p. 342), potentially posing an existential risk to our species and planetary dominance (Bostrom, 2002). However, Good argued that as long as humans can keep the machine under control, we need not fear artificial intelligence (1966, p. 33). Of course, although it is not elaborated on in this work for obvious

Image 7.1 Deepfake depicting the alleged aftermath of an alleged Israeli attack on Palestinian soil. Source: fastcheck.cl

reasons, artistic professions have viewed the introduction of these technologies into their workspaces with apprehension, as the popularisation of AI calls into question the role of human creativity in society (Fernández, 2023, p. 344).

7.4 Digital Divide and the Search for the Truth

Just as fact-checking exists to verify the accuracy of information, the development of deepfake images and their dissemination on the Internet has led to the creation of methods to verify the authenticity of images. One of the most popular methods is Error Level Analysis (ELA), a digital tool that allows the recognition of "areas in the image with different compression levels" (Niteesh, 2021, p. 3). Just as there are systems to detect deepfake audios (Zhang et al., 2024) or deepfake videos, there are multiple systems to try to detect synthetic images, but they require training in new technologies.

The problem with these types of tools is that they require training in new technologies, making access to truth even more challenging for individuals lacking digital competencies. It's important to remember that the digital divide is a problem in contemporary societies—specifically in the knowledge society (Cabrero & Ruiz-Palmero, 2018, p. 17)—with a certain level of technological development and an ageing population that has not adapted to these changes. Its effects are so significant that in 2005, it was listed among the five major obstacles hindering the advancement of the knowledge society (UNESCO, 2005, p. 36).

The situation worsens when we consider that we live in a world where people from disadvantaged groups have fewer opportunities to participate in the virtual world (Segura & Conejero, 2023, p. 815). Understanding this as a social scheme where "the younger population demonstrated a higher detection rate despite the trivial accuracy score" (Preu et al., 2022, p. 0552) highlights the particularly affected group: the elderly (Van Deursen & Van Dijk, 2014).

The integration of these groups becomes even more important if we understand that the presence of technology determines social relationships in the digital life world (Villalobos-Antúnez et al., 2023, p. 13). Finding a solution to this problem is particularly urgent considering that generative artificial intelligence for images may erode our ability to distinguish between real and artificial images (Fernández, 2023, p. 343).

7.5 Conclusion

In this study, a palpable reality is exposed: after conducting a thorough investigation into methodologies that detect images produced by artificial intelligence, there is no proven system that prevents digitally vulnerable individuals from being deceived by this new way of distorting reality. Finding a solution is particularly urgent when deepfakes can impersonate identities for defamatory or criminal purposes, or when unreal images are reproduced as if they were true.

Since these compositions do not rely on words—setting them apart from memes—there are verbo-lingual elements in propaganda discourse highlighted by Dimitrov et al. (2019, pp. 6606–6607) that must be considered, specifically those focusing on communication through images. Therefore, current circumstances not only underscore the necessity of fact-checking platforms—they are the most crucial detectors of fake news—but also suggest the importance of creating identification methods for AI compositions that are accessible to the less specialised public, outside scientific or research environments.

Therefore, the current circumstances not only highlight the necessity of fact-checking platforms—they are the primary detectors of fake news—but also emphasise the importance of developing identification methods for AI compositions that are accessible to the general public, especially those outside scientific or research environments. This would help mitigate the spread of misinformation and enhance public awareness of the potential manipulation through synthetic media, which relies heavily on visual elements rather than textual content, distinguishing it from memes.

The next step for this group is to shape this methodology and implement it among the users of Santa Cruz Vital, a project by the Santa Cruz de Tenerife City Council driven by the Municipal Institute of Social Care, IMAS. The initiative focuses on providing active aging proposals involving around five hundred elderly individuals, with whom several sessions will be conducted—creating subgroups of 20 to 30 people is advisable—to test the effectiveness of this system.

References

Abdullah, S. M.; Cheruvu, A.; Kanchi, S.; Chung, T.; Gao, P.; Jadliwala, M.; Viswanath, B.; & Tech, V. (2024). An analysis of recent advances in deepfake image detection in an evolving threat landscape. ArXiv:2404.16212, 1–19. doi: https://doi.org/10.48550/arXiv.24.16212.

Aminulloh, A., Qorib, F., Fianto, L., & Dwinanarhati, E. (2022). Propaganda al political memes on social media in the 2019 Indonesian presidential election. *Journal of Islamic World and Politics, 6*(2), 342–365.

Ballester, L., Dosil, M., Villena, A. & Testa, G. (2023). La nueva pornografía "online" y los procesos de naturalización de la violencia sexual. In A. Gutiérrez García (Coord.), *Una mirada interdisciplinar hacia las violencias sexuales* (233–250). Ediciones Octaedro.

Bañuelos, J. (2020). Deepfake: Images in times of post-truth. *Revista Panamericana de Comunicación, 1*(2), 51–61.

Barrientos, A., Piñeiro, T., & Porto, D. (2024). Fake images, real effects: Deepfakes as manifestations of gender-based political violence. *Revista Latina de Comunicación Social, 82*, 1–29.

Bostrom, N. (2002). Existential risks. *Journal of Evolution and Technology, 9*(1), 1–31.

Cabrero, J., & Ruiz-Palmero, J. (2018). Technologies of information and communication for inclusion: Reformulating the "digital gap". *International Journal of Educational Research and Innovation, 9*, 16–30.

Cerdán, V., & Padilla, G. (2019). Historia del "fake" audiovisual: "deepfake" y la mujer en un imaginario falsificado y perverso. *Historia y Comunicación Social, 24*(2), 505–520. https://doi.org/10.5209/HICS.66293

Chalmers, D. J. (2017). The virtual and the real. *Disputatio: International Journal of Philosophy, 9*(46). https://doi.org/10.1515/disp-2017-0009

Chalmers, D. J. (2022). *Reality+: Virtual worlds and the problems of philosophy*. Penguin.

Chen, P., Zhao, L., Oiao, Y., Ding, H., & Cui, X. (2024). Multimodal visual-textual object graph attention network for propaganda detection in memes. *Multimedia Tools and Applications, 83*, 36629–36644. https://doi.org/10.1007/s11042-023-15272-6

Cortés, J. (2019). La alfabetización informacional, bastión en tiempos de la posverdad. *Bibliotecas. Anales de Investigación, 15*(3), 412–420.

Davison, P. (2012). The language of internet memes. In M. Mandiberg (Ed.), *The social mediareader* (pp. 120–136). New York University Press.

Dimitrov, D., Ali, B. B., Shaar, S., Alam, F., Silvestri, F., Firooz, H., Nakov, P., & San Martino, G. (2019). Detecting propaganda techniques in memes. In C. Zong, F. Xia, W. Li & R. Navigli (Eds.), *Proceedings of the 59th annual meeting of the association for computational linguistics and the 11th international joint conference on natural language processing (Volume 1: Long Papers)* (pp. 6603–6617). Association for Computational Linguistics. doi: https://doi.org/10.48550/arXiv.2109.08013

Fernández, J. (2022). Realidad artificial. Un análisis de las potenciales amenazas de la Inteligencia Artificial. *VISUAL REVIEW. International Visual Culture Review/Revista Internacional de Cultura Visual, 9*(2), 335–347. https://doi.org/10.37467/revvisual.v10.4607

Figueroa, H. A. (2024) In E. Morales (Coord.) Información y crisis (81–96). Universidad Nacional Autónoma de México.

Franganillo, J. (2023). La inteligencia artificial generativa y su impacto en la creación de contenidos mediáticos. Methaodos. *Revista de ciencias sociales,* 11(2), 1–17. http://dx.doi.org/10.17502/mrcs.v11i2.710

García, G., & López, X. (2020). La verificación de datos en Europa. Análisis de 5 iniciativas europeas: Maldita.es, Newtral, Pagella Politica, Les Décodeurs y BBC Reality Check. *AdComunica, Revista Científica de Estrategias, Tendencias e Innovación en Comunicación, 21*, 235–264. https://doi.org/10.6035/2174-0992.2021.21.12

Garriga, M., Ruiz-Incertis, R., & Magallón-Rosa, R. (2024). Artificial intelligence, disinformation and media literacy proposals around deepfakes. *OBS* Journal, 18*(Special Issue), 175–194.

Gómez, H., & Tamayo, J. L. (2023). Algorithmgraphy as a milestone and phenomenon in the production of still images in the digital era: Resignification of the notion of the photographic image and projection of the medium in a context of image production with artificial intelligence and machine learning. *Visual Review. International Visual Culture Review/Revista Internacional de Cultura Visual, 14*(2), 1–13. https://doi.org/10.37467/revvisual.v10.4607

Good, I. J. (1966). Speculations concerning the first ultraintelligent machine. In *Advances in computers* (Vol. 6, pp. 31–88). Elsevier. https://doi.org/10.1016/S0065-2458(08)60418-0

Gundapu, S. & Mamidi, R. (2022). Detection of propaganda techniques in visuo-lingual metaphor in memes. ArXiv:2205.02937, 1-12. doi:https://doi.org/10.48550/arXiv.2205.02937.

Jacobsen, B. N., & Simpson, J. (2023). The tensions of *deepfakes*. *Information, Communication and Society, 27*(6), 1095–1109. https://doi.org/10.1080/1369118X.2023.2234980

Lavrov, S. (2003). Genuine multilateralism and diplomacy vs the "rules-based order". *Russia in Global Affairs, 21*(3), 104–113.

Mania, K. (2024). Legal protection of revenge and deepfake porn victims in the European union: Findings from a comparative legal study. *Trauma, Violence & Abuse, 25*(1), 117–129. https://doi.org/10.1177/15248380221143772

Manrique, J. L. (2016). Populismo y posverdad, ¿Sólo tendencias? *Inmanencia, 5*(1), 161–165.

Martínez, M. (2023). The revenge porn discourse in the press: A case study of Spanish singer Rosalía and her manipulated images. *Journal of Feminist, Gender and Women Studies, 15*, 94–115.

Niteesh, K., Pranav, P., Vishal, N., & Geetha, V. (2021). Deepfake image detection using CNNs and transfer learning. In *2021 International Conference on computing, communication and green engineering (CCGE)* (pp. 1–6). https://doi.org/10.1109/CCGE50943.2021.9776410

Preu, E., Jackson, M., & Choudhury, N. (2022). Perception vs. Reality: Understanding and Evaluating the Impact of Synthetic Image Deepfakes over College Students. *IEEE 13th Annual Ubiquitous Computing, Electronics & Mobile Communication Conference (UEMCON)*, 0547-0553. https://doi.org/10.1109/UEMCON54665.2022.9965697

Rogers, R., & Giorgi, G. (2024). What is a meme, technically speaking? *Information, Communication and Society, 27*(1), 73–91. https://doi.org/10.1080/1369118X.2023.2174790

Sádaba, C., & Salaverría, R. (2023). Combatir la desinformación con alfabetización mediática: Análisis de las tendencias en la UE. *Revista Latina de Comunicación Social, 81*, 17–33. https://doi.org/10.4185/RLCS-2023-1552

Sanchez, B. (2020). Internet memes and desensitization. *Pathways, a Journal of Humanistic and Social Inquiry, 1*(2), 1–11.

Segura, M. C. & Conejero, E. (2023). Gobernanza y brecha digital durante la COVID-19: el caso español. In K. Álvarez & A. Cotán (Coords.) *Educar, comunicar, sociabilizar en la heterogeneidad* (812–827). Dykinson

UNESCO. (2005). *Hacia las sociedades del conocimiento*. Ediciones UNESCO.

Van Deursen, A., & Van Dijk, J. (2014). The digital divide shifts to differences in usage. *New Media and Society, 16*(3), 507–526. https://doi.org/10.1177/1461444813487

Vega, A., Esquivel, D. C., Barrera, A. C., & Pacheco, C. (2024). La Violencia Sociodigital contra las Mujeres. Atlánticas. *Revista Internacional De Estudios Feministas, 9*(1), 1–31. https://doi.org/10.17979/arief.2024.9.1.9985

Villalobos-Antúnez, J. V., Guerrero-Lobo, J. F., Martin-Fiorino, V., Astudillo-Campusano, P., & Caldera Ynfante, J. E. (2023). Digital culture and the information regime: Political governance in times of democratic system crisis. *Techno Review. International Technology, Science and Society Review, 13*(4), 1–17. https://doi.org/10.37467/revtechno.v13.4817

Wang, S., & Kim, S. (2022). Users' emotional and behavioral responses to deepfake videos of K-pop idols. *Computers in Human Behavior, 134*, 107305. https://doi.org/10.1016/j.chb.2022.107305
Zhang, X., Yi, J., Wang, C., Zhang, C. Y., Zeng, S., & Tao, J. (2024). What to remember: Self-adaptive continual learning for audio deepfake detection. *Proceedings of the AAAI Conference on Artificial Intelligence, 38*(17), 19569–19577. https://doi.org/10.1609/aaai.v38i17.29929

Lucas Morales Domínguez, PhD in Arts and Humanities from Universidad de La Laguna (2023). Master's in Communication Sciences from Universidad de La Laguna (2015). Bachelor's in Journalism from Universidad de La Laguna (2013). Higher Technician in Illustration, Design, and Plastic Arts (2006). University professor at the School of Tourism of Santa Cruz de Tenerife (2014–2018). Currently, a substitute professor at Universidad de La Laguna in the Journalism Degree at the Faculty of Social Sciences and Communication and director of the Canarian Foundation for the Study and Promotion of Narrative in Images. Author of articles in indexed journals such as Estudios del Mensaje Periodístico or Trípodos, among others. Additionally, he has participated in educational innovation projects involving radio development in the classroom in the digital newspaper Periodismo ULL, edited by the Communication Laboratory of the Universidad de La Laguna. His research interests include film studies, orientalism, and narrative in images.

José Luis Zurita Andión, PhD in Information Sciences from the University of La Laguna (2011) and a Bachelor's in Geography and History from the same academic institution (1993). He coordinates the Communication Laboratory (research group) at the University of La Laguna, teaching as an assistant professor in the Journalism Degree at the Faculty of Social Sciences and Communication, as well as in the Master's in Communicative Innovation in Organizations. Since 2016, he has directed the digital newspaper Periodismo ULL, a unique educational innovation project in Spain. On it he works the informative production within the framework of new narratives and communication technologies. He is part of the Permanent Educational Innovation Group on Gender Inclusive Language at the University of Málaga, and the research group Language and Press, also at the University of Málaga. He has had academic stays at the universities of Málaga, Austral (Argentina), and Autonomous University of Baja California (Mexico). As the author of three books, scientific and outreach articles, as well as book chapters, he also researches entrepreneurship in the communication field after promoting the creation of four companies.

Malgorzata Kolankowska, PhD—graduated from Spanish Philology and Journalism at the University of Wroclaw. Author of the book Red and Black. Polish media discourse on Chile and of various papers on spanish and polish media and culture. She is interested in interdisciplinary studies concerning relations between media, culture and cultural and collective memory. The translator and the author of anthology titled A Portray of a Woman in short stories of ten Spanish Writers. She has organized various congresses related to polish, spanish and latin american culture and has participated in many projects promoting spanish literature in Poland.

Chapter 8
Generative Artificial Intelligence in Audiovisual Screenwriting

Mario Rajas and Manuel Gértrudix

8.1 Introduction: The Future Is Yesterday

Generative artificial intelligence (Generative AI, GenAI or GAI) is revolutionizing the production of audiovisual content. An unstoppable transformation is changing daily, at breakneck speed, with the continuous irruption of technological advances, disruptive emerging processes, and new innovative techniques and languages for the creation of images and sounds (Hinojosa Becerra et al., 2024). As AI is a field of research that is in constant evolution (Franganillo, 2023), when talking about AI, one must be aware of a series of conceptual and methodological obstacles.

Firstly, as a technology that is constantly evolving, AI is in reality at a very early stage of development—however surprising and ground-breaking the milestones that have already been achieved in the specific field of media may seem—in one of the first steps of a supposedly relentless upward trajectory. The state of the art that will be achieved in the not-too-distant future will have little to do with the partial and limited progress that has been achieved up to this point (McKnight, 2021). Therefore, it is more interesting to ask questions about the capability of AI in the future than to try to provide static answers about an outdated present that seems to become a distant past at any moment.

Secondly, analyzing a phenomenon as multi-layered as AI applied to audiovisual production requires the interplay of many fields of knowledge (Renzi et al., 2023). On the one hand, there are complex branches of AI: machine learning, natural language processing, computer vision, cognitive robotics, or expert systems. Each of these branches, in turn, comprises a significant number of areas or modalities. For

---

M. Rajas (✉) · M. Gértrudix
Communication Sciences Faculty, Department of Audiovisual Communication and Advertising, Rey Juan Carlos University, Madrid, Spain
e-mail: mario.rajas@urjc.es; manuel.gertrudix@urjc.es

A. Baraybar-Fernández et al. (eds.), *The AI Revolution*, Research Series on Responsible Enterprise Ecosystems, https://doi.org/10.1007/978-3-031-80411-3_8

example, in the field of machine learning alone, there are: supervised learning, unsupervised learning, reinforcement learning, deep learning, and neural networks, among which generative adversarial networks stand out in particular (Nawaz et al., 2023).

On the other hand, the areas in which these insights have direct implications when applied to mass media are no less heterogeneous (Thorne, 2020): the production and distribution of visual and audio content, industrial, commercial, and professional labor structures, aesthetic and cultural transformation, copyright and intellectual property, legislative frameworks and ethical foundations, etc. (García-Regalado & Carballo-Valverde, 2022; Zelcer, 2023).

For this reason, this research on the application of AI to audiovisual scriptwriting has taken into account both the urgency of thinking about the future and the need for an interdisciplinary approach that combines advances in communication sciences and in other fields such as data science, software engineering, robotics, or cybersecurity (Dayo et al., 2023; Zhao et al., 2022).

The aim is therefore to analyze the ability of AI to be involved into the creative processes of audiovisual writing and to offer innovative results in the creation of scripts for all types of film, television, or multimedia formats. The specific objectives are, on the one hand, to describe the characteristics of AI as a "scriptwriter" and the actions that can be carried out with it and, on the other hand, to open up the creative, employment and ethical debates that the crucial inclusion of the AI in audiovisual writing workflows raises among professionals.

8.2 Generative Artificial Intelligence in the Audiovisual Creation Process

Generative artificial intelligence is a branch of AI that consists of the creation of original content in written, audio, or visual form (Bringsjord et al., 2016). Based on algorithms, natural language processing, and machine learning models, it can process large amounts of data to generate new content: literary texts, musical themes, illustrations, videos, podcasts … (Gértrudix & Rubio Tamayo, 2023).

Depending on the result of a written request in the form of an instruction or *prompt*, three types of GAI can be distinguished: Text GAI (represented by applications such as ChatGPT, GPT-4, Copilot, or Bard); image GAI (Midjourney, BlueWillow, Dall-E3, Lens Go, Stable Diffusion, Leonardo, or Firefly) or video GAI (Gen-3, D-ID, Lumen 5, HeyGen, Synthesia or Sora). Similarly, multimodal GAIs are those that combine text with audio, audio with image or text and audio with image as input and output.

AI can be used in every phase of the audiovisual process: screenwriting, art direction, acting performance, direction of photography, sound design, editing/montage, and visual effects composition (Gobet & Sala, 2019). Although most authors (Trach, 2022) focus on the study of the effective end result of content production, i.e. illustrations and finished films and their impact on the viewer, the analysis of the preceding components and creative phases is not considered to the same extent, especially the scriptwriting phase that finally leads to the audiovisual or multimedia product.

Due to the large number of languages, programs, platforms, and versions that are being integrated into the living ecosystem of GAI, in this article, although we will mention the most widely used AI applications for the audiovisual scriptwriting field, we will not focus specifically on any of them, but rather summarize the technical features, creative possibilities, and enhancement opportunities they all offer as a set of tools in development. The unstoppable evolution of the possibilities of technology that is too young—the first project written by an AI, *Sunspring* (Oscar Sharp), in which three interpreters interact with each other with disjointed and meaningless dialogues, dates only from 2016—makes it advisable not to limit ourselves to the state of the art and to open ourselves to observating future trends and lines of research.

8.3 The Artificial Scriptwriter

The AI applied to audiovisual writing is based both on specialized software (Squibler, Genario) and on the integration of certain functions in existing script formatting software (Story Architect, Celtx). In both modalities, the most prominent features of AI can be subdivided into four interrelated sections: process management, ideation, writing techniques, and evaluation and communication of results.

8.3.1 Process Management

AI helps to organize the work of writing an audiovisual script. The main advantages in this regard are:

1. It saves time and effort in each phase of the process by automating design and structuring tasks for a given project.
2. Speed in the planning and execution of each task of integral management of the material. An incentive, especially in media that require high production speed, such as television.
3. Its versatility and flexibility make it possible to tackle any type of writing format and genre, be it the creation of content for film, television, video games, social networks, or storytelling in specific contexts (education, science, business, etc.).
4. It can be applied to the entire writing process (from the ideation of a concept to writing the final draft, including the storyboard, treatment, synopsis, logline, tagline, etc.) or only to one of these phases or specific behaviors (designing the bible of a series, polishing the dialogue).

5. Helps to collaborate on projects carried out by more than one writer. It virtually connects and organizes the development of a work that requires the concurrence of several remote professionals writing simultaneously.

8.3.2 *Ideation*

The most representative area of the AI applied to audiovisual writing so far is the support in formulating and contrasting new ideas for the development of a script. The most notable benefits are:

1. Instant access to a large amount of information. It is a search engine both for documentation relevant to the writing of the project and for a database of scripts, guidelines, trends, or pre-existing examples—templates, writing prompts, dialogues, etc.—which can be found in a variety of sources available in real time.
2. It helps against "writer's block." It is a reference for methods, mechanisms, and inspiration for possible creative bottlenecks. The various scriptwriting AI applications point out that its tools can combat, as an essential feature, the lack of ideas that can occur during the writing process, especially in the initial stages. AI can spur the author's creativity by helping them in several ways: offering alternatives, new points of view and opposing angles or solving a specific problem that prevents the fluidity of the writing process when faced with the blank page.
3. Creative thinking methods such as brainstorming. It offers a variety of options and multiple combinations, operational solutions to problems or different perspectives that can serve as a basis for the scriptwriters to develop their own ideas or implement to the proposals suggested by the AI to the desired extent.
4. Preliminary analysis for project design. Study of global narrative trends, channels, formats, genres, audiences, markets, or consumption habits summarized in millions of pieces of data. The constant research of the media context is a very powerful tool to approach projects on a solid creative and commercial basis, such as the expected box-office results, the film awards for which the film is eligible of certain types of content by specialized critics and audiences—preferences, demands.

8.3.3 *Writing Techniques*

Undoubtedly, this is the fundamental part of the application of AI in the creation of audiovisual scripts. The narrative strategies and procedures that a particular application can bring to scriptwriting are at the center of GAI's role in reinventing media:

1. Apply specific scripting models. It can be based on well-known audiovisual structures—the three acts of the Syd Field-Linda Seger paradigm; the five stages of Robert McKee or the six of Michael Hauge; the fifteen steps of Blake Snyder's

Save the Cat! or classical designs—such as the twelve steps of Christopher Vogler's Hero's Journey or the five of Freytag's pyramid. The AI uses these familiar models which enable the scriptwriter to work according to proven schemes when writing stories for film or television. It is also possible to use previously produced scripts—or simulate the style of a renowned screenwriter—to create new content based on a particular text or author, or to require the integration of specific techniques or narrative figures from these previous works.
2. The writing of the entire script or the elaboration of certain specific content: creation of narrative universes, dramatic architectures, plots, sequences-scenes, characters, dialogues, etc. AI can be used as an integral audiovisual writing tool providing a complete literary script at the end or as a specialized process at a specific moment when a very specific contribution is needed.
3. Editing and rewriting. It is possible to edit the results offered by the AI in both directions or, as we will see below, for the AI to also re-edit the material prepared by the scriptwriter. The AI becomes an assistant that detects possible structural problems, inadequacies or errors in a narrative component, spelling mistakes, linguistic ambiguities or typos. In this sense, the ability to create multiple revised versions of a script is one of the main potential benefits of the new technology.
4. Define a writing style. Whether lexical, syntactic, or grammatical AI can help in the search for vocabulary, adopt different writing styles (poetic, formal, etc.) and provide coherence and uniformity to the style of expression chosen for a given project. The nuances of language—subtexts, tropes—and the visual and sonorous expression of subjects, verbs, adverbs, or adjectives are crucial in this artistic sense.
5. Give an existing text a font format. This means intervening not in the creation of the content, but in the form or expression of it, by adding the standardized components of the script models: headline, description, character, dialogue, stage direction, and transition. Among other things, the American or European format, among others, is applied to a text previously written by the scriptwriter, so that the standardized requirements in terms of font type and size, line spacing, universal indications (V.O., CONT'D, etc.) are met. The idea is to simplify and automate perform a mechanical, uncreative task that is nowadays performed semi-manually with professional script formatting software such as Final Draft, Fade In or the aforementioned Celtx or Story Architect. The ability to customize, adapting or re-editing the formatting done by the AI increases the potential of these formatting tools.
6. Suggest new ways of writing. AI can even go a step further and invent new ways of creating audiovisual scripts by providing innovative ideas in each of its facets. This involves creating disruptive processes, functions, formats, or content that are not currently used—or imagined—in the industry: devising original, multidimensional stories, structures, plots, or characters; formulating truly transformative workflows; reconfiguring traditional format elements and developing new creative models, etc.

8.3.4 *Evaluation and Communication of Results*

Just as AI analyzes existing content during the research or documentation phase of a project, it can also turn the text itself into a source for studies and evaluations at the end of the script development phase. Above all, it can be used for:

1. Exhaustive analysis of the work. Feedback on the written script. It includes the elaboration of quantitative reports (data on scenes, characters, percentage of dialogues, etc.) and qualitative reports (critical comments, suggestions for improvement) as well as various checks and final comments on both content and form of expression.
2. Convert text to audio. The AI reads the text aloud in a male or female voice selected by the user. Some video software can also transfer the content of the script to the screen, i.e. they are able to convert the written text into images and sounds.
3. Automatic translation. This entails the ability to create multiple versions in different languages. The AI can also transcribe videos and convert them into text making the appropriate changes and adapting the content to different geographical, cultural, or social contexts.
4. Dissemination of the work, from the registration or submission of the script to the rights entities or screenwriters' unions to the coordination of the work with other departments of the audiovisual production departments. He/she may also be responsible for writing press releases, captions, elaborating metadata for indexing in websites or other SEO strategy tools.
5. Learning tool. The AI fulfills a didactic function by teaching the theory and practice of screenwriting using the materials created. As the AI learns, it can teach audiovisual script students the basics and details of the craft. The AI can be adapted to any learning level—beginners or experienced professionals—and to any specific training context.
6. Scientific communication: each AI project contributes to dissemination of the tools, datasets, etc. used. The technological, industrial, or artistic knowledge generated is transferred to society beyond the result of the audiovisual work.

8.4 Functionalities and Parameters

Whether in the management of the process, the generation of ideas, the writing procedures, or the evaluation and communication of the results, AI applied to audiovisual scripts offers a range of operational functionalities, technical-expressive parameters, and customizable settings that make this advanced content creation technology truly a digital tool with unlimited potential.

On the one hand, each of the aspects mentioned above is fully configurable. The customization of processes or methods as well as of techniques or creative resources make AI a tool with great adaptability to the specific and changing needs or conditions of a project. Thus, the length/duration, tone of voice or style, to name three very relevant narrative decisions among many others, can be highly varied. For example, opt for a more emotional or neutral text or choose the level of creativity—on a scale of 1 to 10 for some software—you want the AI to adopt based on the prompts or text instructions included in the platform.

This adaptability begins in the documentation phase of a project: the GAI classifies, tags, and retrieves a huge amount of data that can be used in very heterogeneous ways during the genesis of a script. From this moment on, the author will have to make many decisions regarding the use of the AI: whether to involve it as a personal assistant or *chatbot*; whether to relegate it to the function of "autocompleting" certain passages of the script such as dialogue sentences or descriptions; whether to let it interfere—to a greater or lesser extent—in the most central and creative aspects of the script—informational-emotional progression, capturing the viewer's interest and attention, character transformation arcs, etc.; or whether it allows him to correct, edit, or rewrite the work alone or as an additional process to the previous ones.

In this sense, AI can act, in a combined way, as a mirror, returning results that reflect the interests, tastes, or habits of the scriptwriter; or as a window that provides access to results, perspectives, or creative visions that are different or opposite to one's own.

In short, the different AI applications aimed at the audiovisual script become laboratories where to experiment functions and tools that, at a dizzying pace, are being incorporated to the catalog of artistic and technical possibilities offered to the writer. In the current phase of technological development, each software or platform is constantly being updated, perfecting routines and procedures, improve usability and surprise with powerful advantages that are themselves precursors to new discoveries.

The difficulty is deciding which application to learn. The list is endless and constantly renewed: Squibler, Genario, Writer Hand, White Cream, Boords, Simplified, ScripAI, Vondy, ToolBaz, Nolan AI, Hypotenuse AI … The competition among them forces developers to innovate and integrate as many advantages as possible and to be very precise in the technical improvements they offer. For the user, the challenge of knowing and managing so many tools is enormous.

8.5 Open Discussions

Like any breakthrough technology, GAI presents a series of heterogeneous challenges and issues that need to be addressed from a multidisciplinary perspective. The discussions will take place along four main axes: technological, labor, legislative and, above all, creative.

The most important technological questions that need to be resolved are the following: Will GAI, applied to audiovisual scriptwriting, really reach an advanced stage of development or will it be merely a tool with more or less practical functionality? From considering it a simple inefficient autocompletion or chat tool to defending a global, holistic vision of the supposedly unlimited capabilities of GAI, the different authors consider that, within these two extremes, the technology will gradually opt for certain functions—search engine, analysis tool, collaboration support, etc.— and abandon others that are not relevant. On the other hand, as already mentioned, the proliferation of platforms, applications, software—independent or integrated in turn into other programs, which are constantly being updated—brings with it certain challenges in terms of standardization of processes, comparing the quality of the content produced and development of learning curves. For a professional writer, familiarizing themselves with such a large amount of software can be a tedious and daunting task.

In this sense, the concern on the labor market is quite understandable. The screenwriters' strike supported by the Writers Guild of America (Fierro Rodríguez, 2023) is an example of the risks that a technological revolution such as AI entails. In addition to the change in professions—screenwriter, analyst, agent, etc.—there are other questions related to the change in the production model and the reconfiguration of the industry: Will the current process of phases be divided into pre-production–production–post-production disappear? Will some trades be integrated into others? Will AI be the decision-maker and the scriptwriter the tool to execute it? How can we talk about labor or trade union rights when such important concepts as working hours or the length of the working day are being changed? Who will appear in the credits?

Thirdly, both national and supranational governments—above all the European Union—are trying to regulate wherever they can. The laws or regulations that might accompany the evolution of GAI also suffer from the problem of the speed of change, but attempts are being made to ensure that any new regulation is not reactive but anticipates possible future developments. The main debates in this area revolve around authorship of the script, intellectual property and copyright; the use of pre-existing sources without explicit authorization; plagiarism, disinformation, or *fake news*; confidentiality, privacy, and anonymity; or professional ethics and deontology. The fact that writing a screenplay is an initial phase of the production process and not a final result that will be broadcast on the screen like a film or a video game requires legislation that does justice to its specific nature.

Finally, the most relevant questions raised by AI are concern creativity in screenwriting: Does AI enhance the originality of works, or does it kill them? Does its own DNA contain clichés, stereotypes or conventional formulas or, on the contrary, is it capable of going far beyond the usual channels in aesthetic and narrative terms? Does AI write with bias, with prejudice, under conditioned cultural, social, and political hegemonic visions? Can the writing style approach the diverse literary poetics or will it be limited to the synthetic and codified writing of audiovisual scripts? How much content can be considered *slop* or garbage produced by AI not supervised by humans? The most repeated questions have to do, on the one hand, with the—infinite—saturation of content that can be generated and, on the other hand, with the necessary acceptance by viewers—fulfilled or rejected expectations-of works written by a non-human artifact or device—in line with the Uncanny

Valley Theory: How do we respond to content produced by a non-natural being? To what extent does the percentage of work by the human scriptwriter or the AI matter in the making of a text? How can we recognize what is the work of one or the other?

8.6 Conclusion: Everything to Be Written

In the coming years, the development of AI in the field of audiovisual scriptwriting will lead to changes in all the areas mentioned above. The crucial question is who will make the hundreds of decisions involved in writing an audiovisual project. In other words: Will the screenwriter has the most revolutionary technology invented to date, or will it be the other way round? Will humans ultimately choose which narrative and aesthetic aspects will shape a work or will they merely execute them? Will the writer be replaced, substituted in his most essential creative functions or simply helped, supported by the AI?

While AI learns and trains, the users go through a similar process in reverse: they discover, test, and learn how to use the technology. The AI may not currently be able to have fun or get excited about the work it is doing, nor be able to write so profoundly that it gives a soul, a sense—not only meaning—to the stories it creates; likewise, the user is not yet able to handle the functionalities, some of them barely sketched, functionalities of the AI, but both are called to understand each other, collaborate and join forces in the writing of an audiovisual project. One suggests, the other supervises; one performs tasks, the other provides their need for self-expression … or vice versa!

If the goal is to create quality scripts—documented, coherent, solid, clear, fluid, plausible, interesting, original, unique, exciting—humans and machines are inevitably called to come together and embark on this creative adventure. From solving very specific problems in a text to completing entire seasons of episodes, AI applied to audiovisual writing discovers new ways of seeing the world, leads us to other impressive forms of narration, other genres, other formats, other writing techniques, in short, it opens the mind—of both artificial intelligence and human intelligence—to unimagined ways of telling stories that today can only be imagined or glimpsed. The page is blank: the turning points of this fascinating technology have only just begun to appear on the screen.

Acknowledgments This project is funded by the FlixOlé-URJC Research Chair of Spanish Cinema of Rey Juan Carlos University.

References

Bringsjord, S., Licato, J., & Bringsjord, A. (2016). The contemporary craft of creating characters meets today's cognitive architectures: A case study in expressivity. In J. Turner, M. Nixon, U. Bernardet, & S. DiPaola (Eds.), *Integrating cognitive architectures into virtual character design* (pp. 151–180). IGI Global. https://doi.org/10.4018/978-1-5225-0454-2.ch006

Dayo, F., Dharejo, N., & Memon, A. (2023). Scriptwriting in the age of AI: Revolutionizing storytelling with artificial intelligence. *Journal of Media and Communication, 4*(2).

Fierro Rodríguez, D. (2023). Strike before the liquidity of intellectual property and image rights in Hollywood. *Diario La Ley, 10356*(1).

Franganillo, J. (2023). Generative artificial intelligence and its impact on media content creation. Methaodos. *Journal of Social Sciences, 11*(2). https://doi.org/10.17502/mrcs.v11i2.710

García-Regalado, U., & Carballo-Valverde, Y. (2022). Artificial intelligence for sentiment analysis in video games. *Techno Review. International Journal of Technology, Science and Society, 11*(2), 185–198. https://doi.org/10.37467/revtechno.v11.3823

Gértrudix, M., & Rubio Tamayo, J. L. (2023). Artificial intelligence, communication, art and science: AI as a field of experimental research. *Telos*. https://telos.fundaciontelefonica.com/inteligencia-artificial-comunicacion-arte-y-ciencia/

Gobet, F., & Sala, G. (2019). How artificial intelligence can help us understand. Human creativity. *Frontiers in Psychology, 10*, 1401. https://doi.org/10.3389/fpsyg.2019.01401

Hinojosa Becerra, M., Marín Gutiérrez, I., & Maldonado Espinosa, M. (2024). Artificial intelligence and audiovisual production. In Torres-Toukoumidis, Á., León-Alberca, T. (coords.), *ComunicAI. La revolución de la Inteligencia Artificial en la Comunicación*. Comunicación Social Ediciones y Publicaciones.

McKnight, L. (2021). Electric sheep? Humans, robots, artificial intelligence, and the future of writing. *Changing English, 28*. https://doi.org/10.1080/1358684X.2021.1941768

Nawaz, M., Javed, A., & Irtaza, A. (2023). Convolutional long short-term memory-based approach for deepfakes detection from videos. *Multimedia Tools and Applications, 83*(6). https://doi.org/10.1007/s11042-023-16196-x

Renzi, G., Rinaldi, A. M., Russo, C., & Tommasino, C. (2023). A storytelling framework based on multimedia knowledge graph using linked open data and deep neural networks . *Multimedia Tools and Applications*, *82*(20). doi:https://doi.org/10.1007/s11042-023-14398-x.

Thorne, S. (2020). Hey Siri, tell me a story: Digital storytelling and AI authorship. *Convergence: The International Journal of Research Into New Media Technologies, 26*(4), 808–823. https://doi.org/10.1177/1354856520913866

Trach, Y. (2022). Experience and prospects of artificial intelligence technologies. Application in the film industry. *Digital Platform: Information Technologies in Sociocultural Sphere, 5*(2), 336–344.

Zelcer, M. (2023). Recommender systems in audiovisual streaming platforms: the logics of algorithms. *Revista Mídia e Cotidiano, 17*(2), 10.22409/rmc.v17i2.57130.

Zhao, G., Li, Y., & Xu, Q. (2022). From emotion AI to cognitive AI. *International Journal of Network Dynamics and Intelligence, 1*, 65–72. https://doi.org/10.53941/ijndi0101006

Mario Rajas, Professor of Audiovisual Screenwriting in the Department of Audiovisual Communication and Advertising of the Faculty of Communication Sciences at the Universidad Rey Juan Carlos. His field of research is the narrative, aesthetics and technology of emerging audiovisual media in educational and scientific communication.

Director of the FlixOlé-URJC Research Chair in Spanish Cinema (2022-x) (cinespanol.es) and coordinator of the High Performance Research Group in Digital Communication and Culture—Ciberimaginario of the URJC (http://ciberimaginario.es). He has been Vice-Dean of Technological Infrastructures and Professional Sectors of the Faculty of Communication Sciences (2018–2022). Previously, he was coordinator of the Academic Content Production Unit of the Centre for

Innovation in Digital Education (CIED) of the URJC (2014–2017). He has been recognised by the CNEAI for two 6-year research periods (2009–2015/2016–2021) and one 6-year transfer period (2018). He has participated in 8 national (2 as Principal Investigator) and 2 international competitive research projects, and in 9 educational innovation projects. He has carried out research stays in centres such as the Instituto Tecnológico de Monterrey (Mexico) (2009), the University of California Los Angeles (United States) (2011), the Escuela Internacional de Cine y Televisión de San Antonio de los Baños (Cuba) (2017) or the Universidade Católica Portuguesa (Portugal) (2021), as well as participating in more than 60 academic activities as a speaker at conferences, seminars and workshops related to his field of study.

Manuel Gértrudix, Professor of Digital and Multimedia Communication in the Department of Audiovisual Communication and Advertising of the Faculty of Communication Sciences at the Rey Juan Carlos University, coordinator of the High Performance Research Group in Digital Communication and Culture - Ciberimaginario of the URJC (http://ciberimaginario.es), and co-editor of the scientific journal Icono14. Specialist in digital communication and elearning he has been IP of 8 competitive national and international research projects and has participated in more than 20. He has an extensive scientific production with more than 110 publications including research articles, book chapters and monographs. He has been Vice Chancellor for Quality, Ethics and Good Governance of the URJC (2018–2021), Academic Director of the Center for Innovation in Digital Education of the URJC (2013–2017), Technical Advisor of New Technologies (2003–2007) and Head of Service of distance education of the Ministry of Education (Spain). He has taught at Universidad Complutense de Madrid (1999–2002), Universidad Francisco de Vitoria (1999–2003) and Universidad Carlos III de Madrid (2003–2007). He is a professor of the Doctorate in Innovation, Communication and Educational Technologies of the ESAE of the Latin American Institute of Educational Culture (Mexico). He has realisazed stays of research in the USA at the University of Central Florida and in Scotland at the University of Stirling. He has taught courses in Argentina at the Universidad Nacional de Córdoba, Colombia, at the Universidad del Norte, and at the UDESC in Brazil.

Index

A. Baraybar-Fernández et al. (eds.), *The AI Revolution*, Research Series on Responsible Enterprise Ecosystems, https://doi.org/10.1007/978-3-031-80411-3

MIX
Papier aus verantwortungsvollen Quellen
Paper from responsible sources
FSC® C105338

If you have any concerns about our products,
you can contact us on
ProductSafety@springernature.com

In case Publisher is established outside the EU,
the EU authorized representative is:
Springer Nature Customer Service Center GmbH
Europaplatz 3, 69115 Heidelberg, Germany

Printed by Libri Plureos GmbH
in Hamburg, Germany